Can't
Is Not
an Option

Can't Is Not an Option

My American Story

Nikki Haley

Sentinel

SENTINEL
Published by the Penguin Group
Penguin Group (USA) Inc., 375 Hudson Street,
New York, New York 10014, U.S.A.
Penguin Group (Canada), 90 Eglinton Avenue East, Suite 700,
Toronto, Ontario, Canada M4P 2Y3
(a division of Pearson Penguin Canada Inc.)
Penguin Books Ltd, 80 Strand, London WC2R 0RL, England
Penguin Ireland, 25 St. Stephen's Green, Dublin 2, Ireland
(a division of Penguin Books Ltd)
Penguin Books Australia Ltd, 250 Camberwell Road, Camberwell,
Victoria 3124, Australia
(a division of Pearson Australia Group Pty Ltd)
Penguin Books India Pvt Ltd, 11 Community Centre, Panchsheel Park,
New Delhi—110 017, India
Penguin Group (NZ), 67 Apollo Drive, Rosedale, Auckland 0632,
New Zealand (a division of Pearson New Zealand Ltd)
Penguin Books (South Africa) (Pty) Ltd, 24 Sturdee Avenue,
Rosebank, Johannesburg 2196, South Africa

Penguin Books Ltd, Registered Offices:
80 Strand, London WC2R 0RL, England

First published in 2012 by Sentinel,
a member of Penguin Group (USA) Inc.

1   3   5   7   9   10   8   6   4   2

ISBN 978-1-59523-085-0

Printed in the United States of America
Set in Bulmer MT
Designed by Spring Hoteling

ALWAYS LEARNING   PEARSON

This book is dedicated to my amazing parents, Dr. Ajit Singh and Mrs. Raj Randhawa, who continue to teach me what it means to live my life with strength and grace. To my incredible husband, Michael, who is my hero and the reason I love my life every day. To my children, Rena and Nalin, who love me unconditionally and inspire me every day to want to be a better mom. And to my brothers, Mitti and Gogi, and my sister, Simmi, who will never know how blessed I feel to have grown up as part of the Original Six.

Contents

Contents

Can't
Is Not
an Option

Chapter One
Bamberg

"**I** am the proud daughter of Indian parents who reminded us every day how blessed we are to live in this country."

That's how I began every speech in my campaign for governor of South Carolina. I said it because I *was* proud—I *am* proud—to be my parents' daughter. But I'll confess: I also said it as a warning, a shot across the bow of those who thought they could make being different—my being different or anyone's being different—a disqualifying factor for leadership. I had been down this road before, and I was done with it. My parents were more American than anyone I knew. The fact that I was their daughter had made me stronger, not weaker. My opponents, I thought, might as well know that up front.

We are all, to one degree or another, reflections of our parents. This is true of me more than most. But I use the word "reflection" deliberately. I am only an echo—an imperfect imitation—of my remarkable parents. If I'm tough and determined, it's because of them. If I am impatient and headstrong, well, that's all on me.

My mom and dad, Raj and Ajit Randhawa, were born in the Punjab region of India. Although she lost her father very young, my mother came from a wealthy family. She lived in a six-story house in the shadow of the Golden Temple, the holiest site of the Sikh religion, to which she belongs. Because she didn't trust it anywhere else, her mother kept all of her cash in the mattress on which she slept. Mom had hired help to attend to her every need. Her clothes were custom made for her. She never had to carry her own books to school. At that time and in that place, girls typically weren't educated beyond high school, but Mom went all the way through law school. She was offered the first female judgeship in India but couldn't accept it because her family didn't think it was appropriate. Women just didn't do those sorts of things.

Mom met Dad at a mountain vacation area near Dharamsala in northern India, where Indian families of means would go every summer to escape the heat. The fact that they met at all made their arranged marriage somewhat unusual. Most Indian brides and grooms never get the chance to meet before they marry. But Mom says she saw Dad and thought he was "a good-looking man." My father's father was a commanding officer in a horse-mounted regiment in the British colonial army. He was stationed all over the country, so my father lived most of the year with his uncle. I remember listening with incomprehension as a child when my dad told me he only saw his parents for two months each year, during his summer vacation.

As was customary, my mom's and dad's families decided their children would marry. They were, it turned out, a good match. Like her, he was Sikh, they were both from prominent families, and they were both educated, my mother with her law degree and my father with a master's degree in biology. Nineteen months after they were married, Mom had my oldest brother, Mitti, in the same house she was born in. To this day, Mitti isn't sure if his birthday is September 26 or 27, due to a delay in issuing his birth certificate, so we celebrate both days for him.

Dad wanted to complete his education with a PhD, but at the time, foreign degrees were preferred, so he chose to study at the University of British Columbia in Vancouver, Canada. He left India for the new world with eight dollars in his pocket. A year later, after he had convinced his adviser they wouldn't distract him from his studies, he sent for my mom and Mitti. Coming to Vancouver was a shock for Mom. She left behind a life of privilege in which hired help performed all the household tasks. Now, not only did she have to cook and clean, but she also had to support my father while he was in school. Mom worked three jobs to support her family—at the post office, selling Avon products, and taking care of a special-needs child—all while tending to Mitti and giving birth to a second child, my older sister, Simmi.

My parents left behind a lot when they left India, not just wealth and comfort but also family and friends. They knew America was a place of unlimited opportunity, and they wanted those opportunities for their children, even if it meant starting over. I know they were homesick at times for their native country. But they never ceased to remind us that it had been worth it to leave. America was a place where opportunities couldn't be bought. They knew that here, if you worked hard, you could be as successful as you wanted to be. So after finishing school in Canada, my father looked for a job in the United States. But it was 1969, a bad year to be looking for work in higher education. One day, Dad was on the phone telling a friend from back home that he was thinking about going back to India because he couldn't find work in the States. "You can't go," his friend said. "America is the best country in the world." The next day, my dad's friend called back. The college Dad's friend taught chemistry at, Voorhees College in Denmark, South Carolina, was looking for an associate professor of biology. Dad didn't know a thing about the college or where it was located, but he accepted anyway. When he told his colleagues in Vancouver that he was heading to South Carolina to teach, one of them commented—seriously—that he might get shot before he got his first paycheck.

My mom remembers landing in Columbia when the family first arrived in South Carolina. It was dark. Mom and Dad had been told that Columbia was the capital, the seat of government and the state's most important city. Where were the lights, she wondered? Where were the big buildings? Columbia was a much smaller place back then than it is now, but it was a metropolis compared to where they were headed. Voorhees was a small, mostly minority college with a student body of about seven hundred. Denmark, the city it was located in, wasn't much bigger.

It's difficult to overstate what unusual figures my mom and dad cut in central South Carolina in 1969. There was my mom, tiny and determined, in her traditional sari. And there was my father, tall and proud, in his Sikh turban. From the beginning, their new country showed them both a boundless capacity for acceptance and the ugly residue of a less tolerant time. On the one hand, my father was welcomed as a professor at the college and my mother was given a job teaching sixth-grade social studies. They met a doctor named Michael Watson, who had been the first physician in the area to integrate his office, allowing blacks and whites to mingle together in the waiting room. Dr. Watson would show my parents repeated kindnesses over the years, not the least of which was delivering me three years later in 1972 . Dr. Watson became a lifelong friend of my family.

But South Carolina in the late 1960s had another side as well. When it came time for my parents to find a home, no one would rent to them. Word quickly got around that my father worked at the "black school," and besides that, he and my mom were obviously foreigners themselves. When they finally found a house, they had to buy it, not rent it. And they were told there were conditions: They couldn't entertain black people in it. They couldn't have alcohol in it. And they had to sell it back to the man they had bought it from. It was located in the nearby town of Bamberg, population 2,500.

Bamberg was born in the 1830s as a water tank erected along the newly built railroad between Hamburg on the Georgia border and Charleston on the sea. Over the years, a town sprang up around that water tank. By the time my family got there 140 years later, Bamberg had a courthouse, a school, a fire department, and a Methodist church. The railroad was still there too. But now, instead of just connecting Hamburg and Charleston, the railroad tracks divided Bamberg. On one side lived the black residents, on the other the white.

We were the first Indian family ever to live in Bamberg. In a time and a place that only knew black and white, we didn't fit either category. We weren't dark enough to be black or pale enough to be white. We were brown. That difference—our difference—was an inescapable fact. We coped the only way we knew how: We went into survival mode. We clung to one another tightly. We worked hard. We were respectful to our neighbors. We tried to fit in.

Today, when we refer to our family back then, we call ourselves "the original six." We are all married now with children, and our family is much bigger. But back then we just had one another, the six of us: Mom, Dad, Mitti, Simmi, me, and eventually my baby brother, Gogi. I used to hear my friends talking about spending time with their grandparents and cousins, and I wondered what that was like. It sounded so fun. I knew my parents had had a big extended family back in India, and my love and respect for them only grew when I thought about how they had left all that love and support behind to create a better life for us.

Life as the original six was pretty simple. Mom and Dad were busy at their various teaching jobs, so the kids took care of one another. Mitti is ten years older than me, and Gogi is five years younger. With Simmi and me in between, each child was in charge of the one below him or her.

We didn't know what we didn't have, but we had one another and we made our own fun. We were constantly outside. We played a lot of kickball. We rode our bikes. We swam at the community pool. My sister and I liked to roller-skate in our neighbor's driveway. I grew to love tennis and spent a lot of time playing doubles with Mitti. On the days we were driven inside by the rain or the heat, we played board games or we played school. My mother would give us a stack of books and tell us to amuse ourselves. Some of our other pastimes were less instructional. When I was young, Mitti would torture me with a game he called "the claw." He would stand over me with one hand stretched out in a gnarled, half-clenched fist, pretending it had a mind of its own and was going to attack. He could get me to do anything by threatening me with the claw.

By the time I was four, thanks to all the books and playing school, I was able to read, I could write in cursive, and I was pretty good at math. Starting school, then, was easy for me. I remember loving kindergarten at Bamberg Elementary. I loved all the arts and crafts and having so many different kids to play with. But even then, during that first stress-free year of school, I was forced to come face-to-face with how different I was from my classmates. At Thanksgiving, someone had the bright idea to give me the role of Pocahontas in the school play. To this day, I'm not sure what my teachers were thinking. Did they realize that I wasn't that kind of Indian? If they did, they never told my classmates. My turn as Pocahontas marked the beginning of a long parade of little boys dancing around me and doing the American Indian hand-to-mouth call. It was annoying. I remember thinking to myself, *Why can't I be a pilgrim?*

Things changed—and not for the better—in first grade. My teacher started sending notes home to my parents. I was distracted, she said, and not paying attention in class. Also, I had acquired an unattractive habit. I would sit there, wandering off somewhere in my mind, and chew my hair. I was tall and awkward, with a face that had not yet grown into my nose. Chewing my hair didn't help make me more attractive to my first-grade classmates or my teacher.

I didn't know it then, but I was bored. The Dick and Jane books we were reading were already below my level. Just about everything my teacher was teaching we had already covered on those rainy days in my living room with my sister and brothers. To make matters worse, my teacher noticed my boredom, and it did not sit well with her. She put me down constantly, saying, "Who do you think you are? What makes you so smart?" On more than one occasion she called me "Miss Smarty Pants" in front of the whole class.

My parents were concerned so they requested a meeting with my teacher. When she sat down with my parents, she complained that I finished my assignments before the rest of the class and spent the rest of the time cutting up. Mom asked her if she could give me extra work or extra reading material to fill the time. But my teacher refused, telling my mother it wasn't her job to keep me academically engaged.

After that meeting, things only got worse at school. One day I was in the classroom while the other kids were out at recess. It was my turn, along with another girl, to tidy up the room. We were cleaning away when someone brought a sheet of paper in and handed it to my teacher. She started reading it and said, "Hum, this is interesting." So the other girl and I went up to her desk. Because I could read, I picked up the memo and started to read it. My teacher snatched it out of my hands. "Listen, Miss Smarty Pants," she yelled. "You can't just go around reading anything you want."

That was enough. The next thing I knew, I was sitting outside the principal's office while my parents met inside. Mom and Dad sat me down that night and told me they had given me a test. Instead of first grade, I should be in third. But because there were only a few weeks left in the school year, they were moving me the next day to a second-grade classroom to ease the transition to third grade the following year.

I was terrified to leave my friends. The next day, as Dad took me to school, I begged him not to make me go to second grade. I felt like I was just starting to get accepted in my first-grade class, and now I would have to start all over. So Dad took me to see the principal, Mr. Ginn, and he said he would sit with me for a while in class until I felt comfortable. That made me feel better.

When I walked into second grade with Mr. Ginn, I was delighted to find that the teacher, Mrs. West, was a very sweet woman with white hair and a comforting face. To this day, she is my favorite teacher. She announced to the class that even though it was the end of the year, I was going to be joining them for the last few weeks. All eyes turned to me. I remember walking to my desk and the girl in front of me, echoing my previous teacher, saying, "What makes you so smart? You don't look smart to me." My only reply was "I don't know."

Starting third grade was tough at first. All the kids knew one another. As a seven-year-old in a class full of eight- and nine-year-olds—and brown to boot—I had trouble being accepted. But I knew it was my job to fix that.

By then I was starting to suspect that my differences from the culture that surrounded me—my religion, my race, and later even my gender—would be a constant issue. I never felt bad about it. I never resented it. I just had to do what my parents had always taught me to do: deal with it. For me that meant focusing on finding the similarities between myself and my friends and avoiding those things that separated us. In practice, this meant becoming adept in the art of finding common ground. When the conversation started to drift to the differences between us, I would quickly switch it to something we could all relate to.

It wasn't always easy. There were any number of topics of life-shattering importance to chattering girlfriends that I had no clue about. Christmas, for one. My parents were and are very serious about their Sikh faith, and when they first arrived, it seemed like everyone in Bamberg worked hard to convert my family. Mom and Dad never abandoned their faith, but they were respectful of those concerned souls who tried to get them to see the light. It seemed like people were always knocking on our door to try to convert us to their religion. Simmi remembers a day when a young boy came up to the house with tears in his eyes and handed her a Bible. "You don't believe in the same God we do and I don't want you to go to hell," he said. She took it and hid it under her pillow. That night, when Mom was tucking her in, she found it and told Simmi, "I want you to read this cover to cover, because there's truth in here." My parents would receive invitations to visit various congregations, and they would take us along. We were exposed early to lots of different faiths. Mom and Dad would always say, "People have different ways of getting to God. The most important thing is that you can't have too much God in your life."

And because they never wanted us to feel left out, Mom and Dad started getting a Christmas tree, decorating it, and putting it up in the family room soon after they moved to Bamberg. My parents always gave presents to our friends at Christmas. (Mitti had to deliver them. Dr. Watson and his family had two lovable but loud Great Danes that always chased him. It was his least favorite part of Christmas.) But Christmas for the family was a pretty humble affair. We would get a couple of presents under the tree and that was it. My friends, on the other hand, had huge, lavish Christmases. Most mysterious of all, they would be visited by a magical, chubby guy named Santa Claus. I simply could not relate. So when everybody started going off about how many gifts Santa had brought them or what he'd left in their Christmas stockings, I would change the subject. I wasn't embarrassed by the fact that my Christmas was different—my parents raised us with too much pride in our heritage for that. I just wanted to fit in.

This habit of finding the similarities and avoiding the differences became very natural to me over time. Eventually I even managed to find my place in third grade. Then one day I went out to play our usual game of kickball with my friends at recess and noticed that everyone was huddled up, staring at me. I walked over and noticed that they were divided into two groups, a black group and a white group. One of the kids in the black group was holding the ball. I got a sick feeling in the pit of my stomach. Whatever this was, it wasn't going to be good. I walked over and said, "Are we playing today?" And one girl said, "We are. You're not."

I was stunned. "Why?" I asked. She replied, "You can play with us, but you have to pick a side. Are you white or are you black?" she replied. I was in a panic. Which side could I choose? What was I? Then I saw the solution: change the subject. I grabbed the ball from the girl and ran as fast as I could to the field. "I'm neither!" I yelled. "I'm brown!" Before I knew it, we were all playing kickball on the playground. I had dodged the issue once again. But something told me it wouldn't be the last time I'd have to.

No amount of artful distraction, of course, could overcome all the challenges we faced in that small town. Many of our neighbors were kind, but there were painful exceptions. After I was born, my mother found herself raising three kids and holding down a full-time job teaching, and she needed some help. The lady across the street baby-sat kids, so my mother asked her if she could watch us during the day. She wouldn't take us. So Mom soldiered on. There was another couple that lived kitty-corner to our house in a trailer. They agreed to watch me, and my mother started taking me over to that trailer every morning before she left for work.

I have no memory of what happened next, but my mother recalls that a few days after I started going to the trailer, she took me out in my stroller for a walk one evening after work. As we approached the path that led to the trailer, I became hysterical, screaming and refusing to go any farther. My mother was mystified, and I was too young to tell her what was wrong. But that night, as she got me ready for my bath, she found out why I had been so upset. My back was covered with deep purple bruises. The woman who lived next door to the trailer—the same woman who had refused to babysit us—later told my mother that she could hear me screaming and crying during the day when I was there. She did nothing. My parents, of course, confronted the couple as soon as they saw my bruises. But the next morning they were gone. They had packed up and left. Years later, when I walked by the trailer, I would still get a sick feeling in my stomach. Until my mother eventually told me what had happened, I never knew why.

We were like that. We didn't talk a lot about the challenges we faced. I don't think any of us wanted to burden the others. We knew we all were going through them. We also knew that life was hard for Mom and Dad. They always provided for us and we never did without. They bought clothes for us twice a year—summer and fall—and we would get a great cake and a gift on our birthdays. We never asked for anything otherwise. We knew we had all we needed. We always knew we were loved.

And to tell the truth, it was my older brother and my father who had the hardest time being accepted in Bamberg, although if you ask them now they will say they never had a problem. Although it is changing, in the Sikh faith men traditionally don't cut their hair. From the time they're little boys, they allow their hair to grow. That's one reason Sikh men wear turbans, to manage their long hair. When Mitti was young, Mom and Dad held to this tradition and didn't cut his hair. Pretty soon, he had long hair that was done up in a bun and covered with the traditional head covering for young boys, called a *juda*. But everywhere he went, people thought Mitti was a girl. Mom would take him to the store and people would say, "What a beautiful girl." She took him to buy clothes and the saleslady showed her to the little girls' department. Mitti says it got so bad that he eventually grabbed a pair of scissors and begged my parents to cut his hair. He was four or five when they gave in to him.

To this day, my dad still proudly wears his turban. At the time I was growing up, most Sikh men in America cut their hair, but not my dad. When we were little, we used to joke that the best part about Dad's turban was that we never lost him. He was easy to spot in a crowd. He's a remarkably tolerant and easygoing guy; he used to joke about it too.

Still, I can't remember a time when I went somewhere with my parents and people didn't stare. "What's that on your head?" they would say. Walking into a restaurant meant hearing people whisper. Walking by a store meant seeing people point.

I can honestly say that I was never embarrassed. I was, however, very sad. My dad is one of the best people I know. He's honest and optimistic. And he loves this country in the way that only a man who gave up a life of comfort and prestige elsewhere can. When I was little, the stares and comments he would evoke instilled in me a kind of quiet sadness. When I was older, it was quiet anger.

One day, when I was about ten, Dad had to go to Columbia, an hour away. This was a big deal when I was growing up, because Columbia was the "big city." I convinced him to let me go with him. On the way, we stopped by a fruit and vegetable stand along the side of the road. There are great ones all over South Carolina, and my parents loved buying produce straight from the farmers whenever they could.

We got out of the car and started filling bags with different things. I was walking along with my dad, pointing out fruits I wanted him to buy. We had the place to ourselves. No other customers were there, just the owners. All of a sudden, two police cars came charging up to the stand. Officers got out of the cars and went and stood by the cash register. I watched them out of the corner of my eye as they talked to the couple at the register and looked back at us. Then I realized they were there because of us. My dad continued filling his bags like nothing was happening. When he was done, he took his basket of fruit over to the register. He said hello to the couple standing next to the policemen and paid for his items.

We got back into the car in total silence. Even then, I knew this was a part of his daily life that he hoped I hadn't noticed. But I did notice, and it hurt.

I still travel that route between Bamberg and Columbia, and that produce stand is still there. When I pass by, I remember what my father so graciously put up with there. And I smile. I smile because I know that the same thing would never happen to him today. South Carolina is a different place. My story is proof of that.

Work was a constant in our lives, especially for my parents. I look back now and I feel bad for them. They never went out on a date. If they couldn't take us with them, they just didn't go. They worked hard to take advantage of the opportunities they knew they had in America, and they did it all for us.

We lived for Sundays, because that was the only day our parents didn't work and our whole family was together. But just because they weren't at their "real" jobs didn't mean there weren't chores to be done. We would start the day with a huge breakfast cooked by Mom. Then we all had to pitch in to do the cleaning that hadn't gotten done all week. Change sheets, vacuum, mop, dust. We never complained. We knew how much Mom and Dad sacrificed. And besides, we were happy just to be together for the day, we original six.

Mom was obsessed with our learning things. She was constantly signing us up for after-school classes. We were rarely consulted beforehand. We would just come home from school and she would summarily inform us that we had dance class in an hour. For me, it was charm school, dance classes, cooking classes, tennis lessons, and Girl Scouts. Some of these classes turned out to be fun. I became, for instance, a tennis fanatic. But others were a disaster. Every Saturday morning, Mom would drop me off at the house of a German lady who lived in Denmark. We would spend the entire day cooking an elaborate meal that I would bring home that night. But it never stuck. I could never cook a meal on my own. The German lady finally brought me back to my mother one day and said, "I can't help her." And she didn't. To this day, if my husband, Michael, didn't cook, my family would never have a home-cooked meal.

One thing I did love was Girl Scouts. The summer after third grade I got to go to Girl Scout camp for a week. It was my first time away from my family, and I missed them terribly, of course. But I had a fantastic time. I loved being around all different kinds of girls from all different backgrounds, religions, and places. There was freedom at camp. But it wasn't the freedom from my family that I prized. It was freedom from judgment. At Girl Scout camp, nobody cared what town you came from or who your family was. We were just friends having fun. Suddenly, all the pressure was gone and I could let my guard down. It was the best week I had ever had.

When I got back home, all I could talk about was Girl Scout camp.

I drove my parents crazy telling them how great it was and how much I wanted to go back. When summer approached after fourth grade, I kept reminding my parents I needed to sign up to go back to camp. I was a total nuisance about it, dancing around the house and constantly reminding everyone that I was going back to Girl Scout camp.

She's different now, but my mom was not a very emotional person when we were growing up. She kept her emotions to herself, and we were expected to do the same. We had a loving household, but we never told one another "I love you" or hugged much. Crying was very much frowned upon. If we did cry, we were told to get a glass of water and go to our room. Today, as an adult and a mom, I understand what my parents were trying to do. They wanted us to be tough. They knew that we would face hardships and obstacles in life, and they wanted us to be prepared. So their philosophy was that you don't complain about problems, you *do* something about them. And when you decide to do something, be the best at it and make sure people remember you for it.

I think back now and realize that my mother didn't give voice to her emotions because she didn't have to. She could do amazing things with just her eyes. All she ever had to do was give us that look of disappointment or anger and we would literally freeze with guilt.

Take report cards, a typically traumatic event in an Indian household. I could be an uninspired student. If I liked something, I excelled at it, but if I was bored, I coasted. So when I brought home a report card with anything less than a *B*, which sometimes happened with subjects that weren't math, I dreaded showing my parents. I would stress about it all day. But when I look back on it, I don't know why I bothered. My mother always did the same thing, no matter what was on my report card. She would put her glasses on, look at the report card, look up at me with her serious eyes, and say, "Well, if you're happy with this then I am."

Ouch. The guilt! She might as well have taken a dagger to my heart. She was pushing me to set higher standards for myself. My parents never punished us—they didn't need to. They used high expectations, encouragement, and, yes, guilt, to have us set standards of excellence for ourselves. When we failed, their disappointment was punishment enough. We knew how hard they worked for us. They devoted everything to us. We wanted to work hard for them in return.

On Sunday afternoons, after the cleaning was done, Mom would take out her bankbooks and do the family finances. One day she asked me to come sit beside her. I sat down and I saw something I had never seen before. She had tears in her eyes. I didn't know how to react. And then her voice started to shake and her lip started to quiver. "I'm sorry," she said. "I know you won't understand this, but Dad and I can't afford to send you to camp this year."

The pain in my mother's eyes was something I will never forget. I knew, even then, that showing this kind of weakness and vulnerability was difficult for her. I knew that her pain was real. I looked at her without thinking and said, "That's okay! I didn't want to go anyway. It really isn't that great of a camp." She gave me a hug and started to cry.

I was lying, and she knew I was lying. She sat with me for a moment, and then suddenly she got up. "Come on!" she said, and she took me outside. It was drizzling. She grabbed my hand and we started running in the yard. The more it rained, the harder we played. We exhausted ourselves and collapsed in a muddy, wet heap. I loved it. I loved the time she and I had together that day. All the disappointment I had about not going to camp went away that day in the rain. I hope her sadness went away too. We never discussed that day again, but it is one I will always remember. I never asked to go to camp again.

During my campaign for governor, a reporter from the *New York Times* interviewed my sister Simmi about our life growing up in Bamberg. The reporter had heard a story about Simmi and me as four- and eight-year-old contestants in the Wee Miss Bamberg pageant. It quickly became one of the stories the media most liked to repeat about me. For too many of them, it confirmed their preconceived notions of life in the South, particularly in the small-town, rural South of Bamberg, South Carolina.

To this day I'm not sure why my mom decided it was a good idea to enter Simmi and me in the pageant. We weren't a family that put a lot of stock in those kinds of things. But I remember I wore a ruffly white dress. My "talent," such as it was, was singing. And my song was "This Land Is Your Land." I remember my brother Mitti playing in the band below the stage as I sang my song. He watched me and started laughing when I forgot the words.

After all the little girls had performed, they lined us all up on the stage. The little white girls were on one side, the little black girls were on the other, and Simmi and I were in the middle. The pageant traditionally had two winners, a black queen and a white queen. But before they revealed who the winners were, the organizers of the pageant said they had an announcement to make. They called Simmi and me out of line and said, "We don't have a place for you." Then they thanked us and handed us gifts. I got a beach ball. I didn't understand. I thought they were giving me a present because everyone liked my song. I remember thinking that when I got home, I was going to rub it in my brother's face for laughing at me.

The beach ball was a disqualification gift. What Simmi understood—and every adult in that auditorium understood—but I didn't, was that my sister and I didn't fit into either of the categories (black and white) by which the pageant judged the winners. Not wanting either race to get upset, the judges disqualified us. I remember being happy that I was able to sing my song. Besides, I loved my beach ball. My parents praised us when we got home and said how great we were. But other than that, we never talked about the incident again.

Many people have found this story shocking, and I suppose to someone who hasn't seen it in context it is. But I do see it in context, and I see it differently. My family and I have some disheartening stories, but every family does. What matters isn't the stories themselves; it's how the stories end.

The year after Simmi and I were disqualified from the pageant, the lady next door, who had originally recommended that my mom enter us in the contest, said she thought we should compete again. I don't know if she hadn't heard about what had happened to us or what. But my mother told her in no uncertain terms that as long as the pageant was segregating the little girls who competed in it, her girls would never have another thing to do with it.

Yes, I was disqualified from the pageant, but the same town that disqualified me was the one that accepted me into a Girl Scout troop, helped my dad get a job in a community college, and helped my mom get a job as a sixth-grade social studies teacher. Over time that town, Bamberg, adopted us as its own. It was a place where I saw firsthand neighbors helping neighbors. I saw the power in the goodness of people doing for one another in good times and bad. Bamberg was a town of faith, values, and patriotism, a town that supported and comforted us when my brother was deployed and fought in the Persian Gulf War.

That was the story I wanted to tell the press. The wonderfully, uniquely American story of a small southern town that accepted an Indian family despite our cultural differences. Was it a perfect place? No place is. But the town of Bamberg showed us that it too could change, and that says more about South Carolina and about America than an awkward day at a kids' pageant.

I don't think I fully realized how much South Carolina has changed since the days of that pageant until I ran for governor. During the campaign, I noticed that my dad would always stand in a corner at events he attended. I wanted everyone to see my parents and how proud I was of them. But I understood why he hid in the corner. He was always concerned that the fact that he looked different would hurt my chances in the campaign. And while it's true that some tried to make our difference a disqualifying issue, they didn't succeed. In the end, my fellow South Carolinians loved that we knew the greatness of the American Dream just as much as anyone born here could—and maybe more, because my parents had come from a place where they couldn't dream such dreams.

The shining moment for me came on inauguration day. On the platform for the swearing-in were all of South Carolina's living former governors, constitutional officers, judges, and dignitaries, and me, Michael, and the kids. And right there, for the whole world to see, in the front row of the platform, were my dad and mom.

I am the proud daughter of Indian parents who reminded me every day how blessed we were to live in this country. At long last, my parents were right where they deserved to be.

Chapter Two
Business School

We didn't talk about politics or government in our house when I was growing up. That may sound strange coming from someone who is best known for my time in public service, but it's true. Who I am was shaped by the people and places I knew growing up, not by ideology or political theory. I learned independence by refusing to be an outsider in my own community. I learned integrity by watching my parents succeed in America. I learned compassion by feeling how much ignorance hurts and seeing how understanding heals.

I never thought of a life in politics. It was a world I knew nothing about and didn't care to. From what I could tell, politicians were people on TV who claimed to be working for us but too often seemed to be busy promoting themselves. In school, being in student government or even taking a political science class was never for me. Instead, I thought I would have a future in business. I always loved numbers, and in the world of business, numbers tell stories that are fascinating to me. Looking back, it's clear to me that my real preparation for my future life began in 1976, when I was four and my mother opened her business.

As usual, my mom's motivation for starting a small business was us kids. She had left everything she had back in India, and she was concerned about the inheritance she would leave us. So after seven years of teaching sixth grade in Bamberg, and without any background in business or any real experience, Mom taught herself how to be a small businesswoman.

She started small—as businesses typically do—and close to home. *In* our home, as a matter of fact, in our living room. She was expecting my little brother Gogi at the time, but she wanted to expose the people of Bamberg to more exotic, international wares, so she opened a gift shop of treasures imported from all over the world. At first she would invite people over to examine her items and buy if they were so inclined. When that took off, she rented a room in a shopping plaza to run her business out of. And when that took off, she purchased and opened her first store.

Aside from making money and bringing some international flare to Bamberg, Mom's strategy in opening the store was to keep her kids close. To her way of thinking, it was better for us to be at the store every day after school than out getting in trouble somewhere. Mitti was busy with two paper routes and a part-time job in a nursing home, but the rest of us worked at the store. My sister and I had the job of dusting the display shelves. I remember vividly how we used to finish a shelf and Mom would come over and run her finger along it and then wipe her finger on one of our shirts. She always—always!—managed to find some dust. Then, as with the report card, she would give us a look that said, "Is this the best you can do?" It was maddening, but it was effective. We learned then that if you're going to do something, do it right or don't do it at all.

My sister, Simmi, is the artistic one in our family. She quickly took to putting together displays in the store that revealed a real eye for fashion and design. But none of that interested me. Once again I was bored. And once again I found myself, after the painstaking dusting was done, chewing my hair and wandering around.

Then one day my mother's bookkeeper, Miss Joyce McMillan, announced that she had taken another job and was leaving. After weeks went by without a replacement being found, she confronted my mother. "Raj," she said. "It's really time. We've got to find out who it is you want me to train to take over when I leave." I remember I was walking out of the little kitchen that was adjacent to Miss Joyce's office when my mom grabbed my arm. She stood me in front of the bookkeeper and said, "I want you to train her."

Miss Joyce laughed. "Her? Raj, you can't be serious. She's twelve!"

"If you teach her, she can do it," my mom replied.

So Miss Joyce trained me. Mom would do the bankbooks, and I did the taxes and everything else. Mom paid me, of course, but she kept every other paycheck because I was earning my "keep." I was writing checks for the business and keeping the general ledger when I was thirteen years old. I told my friends I worked in the store after school, but we never discussed exactly what I did. It wasn't until I went to Clemson and studied accounting that I realized that all twelve- and thirteen-year-olds aren't versed in the business tax code.

I developed a huge love of numbers. When the store's books were off by two cents, I loved finding those two cents. And as my mom's business grew, the challenges grew with it. When I was a teenager, my day-to-day responsibilities centered around making bank deposits, creating sales reports, dealing with accounts receivable, doing the taxes, and maintaining the general ledger. I look back with wonder at how, at such a young age, I saw the business through what was a very transitional time for all small retail businesses. It was a time when cash was tight. Small shops like ours were having to make the transition from keeping their own charge accounts with customers to handing these accounts over to be managed by banks. At the same time, vendors weren't offering the same lines of credit they used to. Before, you had a personal relationship with a vendor, and if you needed an additional thirty days to pay a bill, you could get it. But as cash tightened and the banks became involved in those relationships, that flexibility disappeared.

We had to keep a laser focus on our cash flow. I learned some critical lessons then that have stayed with me as I've moved to public service. I learned early that we couldn't control our revenue stream—we couldn't control who decided to walk in the door of the store and spend their money. All we could control was our expenditures. So we were constantly focused on tightening our overhead. We had to turn over our inventory quickly, even if that meant selling it at a discount. When times were tight, we had to cut back and make tough decisions about how to use our money.

We were a small business trying to compete with giant department stores. That alone was challenge enough. They were big and established and could buy clothing lines at a discount. We couldn't do that. So we had to be creative and look for every competitive advantage. I loved the responsibility and the challenge of that, but I also noticed something. I noticed how hard it was to make a dollar and how easy it was for government to take it away. Government had its hands in literally every aspect of our business. Even as a teenager, that really bothered me. Government charged sales tax to our customers, it charged property tax on the building we were in, it taxed the property and equipment inside the building, and it charged us income tax on what we took in. And none of that counted toward the workers' compensation and other benefits we had to pay. We were struggling just to survive, and government was making it harder, not easier.

In that store, poring over those books, I learned lessons that shaped me for life. By virtue of hard work and sheer will, my mother built the gift shop in our living room into a multimillion-dollar high-end clothing store. I learned more from her example than from anything anyone ever told me in a classroom. I learned the value of discipline and a job well done. I learned that you have to start solving problems before they happen, not after. And I learned that small businesses like ours are the engines that create jobs and grow the economy. Government is the deadweight we all drag behind us.

When it came time for me to go to college, I had my heart set on Clemson. There was a high demand for majors in the textile industry at the time (sadly, that industry died in South Carolina a short time later), and I got a scholarship to go to Clemson to study textile management. Cotton, wool, and silk weren't really my areas of interest, but I thought, *Fine, I'll do it.* I just wanted to go to Clemson.

I remember my parents driving me to campus in August of 1989 and my mom being very quiet. Both she and my dad were concerned, as good Indian parents always are when their children go away. They knew that Clemson was not Bamberg. It was a much larger place, full of young people like me. There was freedom there and a chance to explore. A chance to feel independent and grown up. It was a chance I looked forward to. I had never been out past ten o'clock at night. I had very rarely had sleepovers unless my friends' parents called mine first. I had definitely not been allowed to date. Looking back, I understand why my parents were nervous, but I was very, very excited.

After I got settled in the dorms, a friend from Bamberg, John, came by and said he wanted to introduce my roommate and me to a group of friends. John attended Anderson University, not far from Clemson. It is thanks to John that my very first weekend at Clemson, I met his roommate, Bill Haley. Bill was quiet and cute. Originally from

Ohio, he had moved to Hilton Head Island with his family when he was in ninth grade. We became friends immediately.

Bill was fun and interesting. We spent each day of that weekend together. I really liked him, but it was my first weekend away at school. I had never had the opportunity to date before, and I wasn't ready to like him too much. Fortunately, he helped out on that front when he called me that Tuesday.

"I have a girlfriend," he said. "But I really like you and I enjoyed hanging out." That was it. It was God's way of telling me I could take my time with this one. We saw each other again the next weekend at a party. He was with his girlfriend, but he kept coming over and talking to me. I wanted no part of it, but I thought it was funny that every time she walked away he came over to check on me. Boys.

I guess I shouldn't have been surprised to hear the next week that Bill and his girlfriend had broken up. I can't say I was heartbroken about the turn of events. We started hanging out again.

What I loved about Bill was that he was truly honest. We didn't play games; we didn't try to impress each other. We just laughed a lot. He had had an amazing life. His biological father was an alcoholic who had trouble with the law. His family lived in a house in Ohio with no electricity and no running water. When Bill was three, he and his four siblings were removed from their home by the state. The weekend before his biological mother was going to regain custody of the kids, she got in a car accident and suffered a brain injury. She was no longer able to care for the kids, so Bill and his two sisters were put in foster care in one home, and his older brother and sister went to different homes nearby.

Bill's stories about being in that foster home were like something out of Dickens. It was a big farm where the kids had to work hard all day. At the end of those long days, the adults sat at one table and ate steaks and the children sat at a different table and ate peanut butter and jelly sandwiches. They were never given or offered anything else.

Thankfully, when he was four and his younger sister Lee Anne was three, they were adopted by an amazing couple, Bill and Carole Haley, who couldn't have children of their own. They were from humble backgrounds but were the first in their families to go to college. Carole was a schoolteacher, and Bill was the manager of a steel mill.

Bill and I exchanged childhood stories in an honest but funny way. I was impressed by how much he appreciated the life he had. He knew things could have turned out differently, and he felt blessed that he and his sister had been given a new life. One thing bothered him, though. The Haleys had never been told that there were more than two children to be adopted. His second sister, Rhonda, had been left behind at the foster home. He worried about what had happened to her and whether she was okay. It wasn't until more than fifteen years later that Bill found out his big sister had been adopted by another family, stayed in Ohio, and gotten married and had a daughter. In 1994 her daughter, Sarah, was diagnosed with leukemia and needed a bone marrow transplant. The doctors told Rhonda her siblings would be the best match, so she got the courts to unseal the adoption records. The two oldest kids were still in Ohio. It took a little longer, but she tracked down Bill and her other sister, and within a week they were all together again. Bill was just a baby when he had last seen his older brother and sister—he didn't even remember that they existed. By the time the kids were reunited, Bill's niece had found a bone marrow donor. Still, Bill's amazing story had a double happy ending: He found family he never knew he had, and the niece he had never known found a donor and is now a healthy, happy girl.

I loved how Bill made me laugh, and I was pretty sure the feeling was mutual. He called me a couple days later and told me how much fun he'd had with me. Then came the surprise. "I haven't dated in a while, and I'm not sure I want to jump back into something. There is another girl I like. I would like to date both of you."

I give him points for honesty, but that's about it. So I told him (with a smile, of course), "I think that's great that you're dating again. But I don't date people who also date other people, so why don't you just go date her? Good luck! I hope it works out for you!"

That was the last of that kind of conversation. He never did date the other girl. We, however, went on to date for the next seven years. Little did I know that first weekend at Clemson that my best friend in life would walk through that door, but I thank God every day for him.

In politics people assume that if you're a Republican you're prolife because the party tells you to be. I'm prolife because I get a chance to spend every day with the love of my life knowing that I am blessed that someone saved his life. I would be lost without him.

You may be wondering how "Bill" became South Carolina First Gentleman Michael Haley. After we started dating, I looked at him one day and said, "What's your name?"

"You know it's Bill," he said, puzzled.

"You just don't look like a Bill. What's your whole name?"

"William Michael."

From that point on, I started calling him Michael, and all my friends did the same. When he transferred to Clemson his sophomore year, my friends became his friends, and before we knew it, he was universally known as Michael. Everyone who knew him before I did knows him as Bill, and everyone who met him after I did knows him as Michael.

He looks like a Michael.

Life was good. I was at Clemson. I had met a man. The only problem was, my old nemesis had returned: boredom. Try as I might, I was not interested in textiles. I felt like the kid in the movie *The Graduate* whose would-be father-in-law tells him his future lies in just one word: "plastics." Textiles, like plastics, might have been the wave of the future, but it wasn't for me. I loved math and numbers. So I went home and faced my parents.

"I can't do this," I told my mom. She gave me one of her serious looks. "Okay," she said. "But you get just one chance to change your major. Just one. Don't come back and tell me you're changing your major again." So I changed my major to accounting.

Life at Clemson was eye-opening for me. I had grown up in Bamberg never feeling embarrassed by being different but always being on guard. I was always looking for the ways I was the same as my friends and avoiding the ways I was different. That changed my second year at Clemson. A group of friends and I were walking on campus one day when one of my dear friends made a terrible racial slur about one of the Indian students on campus who didn't speak English very well. I didn't say anything at the time, but I remember going home that night and thinking, *"That insult was aimed at me. If he said that and I didn't say anything, he said that to me—and I just let him do it!"* It was a defining moment. I promised myself then and there that not only would I not stand by and allow anyone to make someone feel bad about being different, but I would also talk more openly about the ways I was different. I had spent so much time changing the subject. Now I talked about being Indian and being raised in a small town, and my friends were fascinated by it. I discovered that my differences actually made me a more interesting friend, a better person, and a better student. All those years I had worried about fitting in. At Clemson I finally realized that my differences were my strengths and gained a new confidence. It didn't take long for that confidence to be tested, however. The first test was the most important one: Michael.

Not long after we met, my parents met Michael for the first time when I gave him a ride from Clemson to Bamberg, which was halfway to Hilton Head, where his parents lived. Before his parents picked him up, Michael met my parents at my mom's store. I introduced him as a friend, but after their meeting, I talked about Michael a lot, I guess, because I remember my mother asking me, "Who is this boy?" My reply was that he was "just a friend," but he wasn't just a friend. He was my first boyfriend. That was the problem.

My parents were better Americans than just about anybody I knew, but they retained their traditional ways when it came to my brothers' and sister's and my getting married. They believed it was their job to choose our spouses. It was hard to argue with them. They came from a culture in India with a less than 1 percent divorce rate. They had come to a culture in America with a divorce rate of over 50 percent. There are important differences between America and India that account for this disparity, but my parents saw it as their duty to make sure that we married well. They believed it was their job to make sure we married someone from the same background, with the same religion and the same education level—just as their families had matched them. They sincerely believed that if they failed to do that, they failed as parents.

I had seen what had happened when my older brother Mitti rebelled against this tradition. Mitti had joined the ROTC in college and had fallen in love with being a soldier. After college he trained at Fort McClellan, Alabama, and then was stationed in South Korea. While he was overseas, my parents went to India and found a girl they thought would be right for him to marry. At first he went along with them, but in the end he broke off the engagement to the Indian girl and married an American girl, Sonya, whom he had met in Alabama. Mitti and I were very close. Even though he was in Korea, I remember feeling a very strong connection with him. I wrote him a letter that tried to express the closeness I felt to him. I quoted the song "Somewhere Out There" and told him that every time I looked at the moon, I felt better knowing he was looking at the same one. It was hokey, but I was twelve, and I was worried about my big brother. Throughout the whole ordeal, I was the go-between, worried about Mitti, worried about my parents.

It was a terrible, terrible time for my family. Mitti and Sonya were married in a small ceremony in Alabama. And when Mitti tried to call and reach out to our parents afterward, they wouldn't speak to him. The year after he was married was the first year we didn't have Christmas at the house. Mom said that if the whole family couldn't be together, we couldn't have Christmas.

My parents eventually reconciled with Mitti and his wife after their daughter, Alyssa, was born and Mitti was deployed to Iraq during Desert Storm. The experience eventually made us a stronger and closer family. But for the rest of us kids, the trauma of the ordeal stayed fresh in our minds as we thought about marriage. My sister was the next to go, and she did everything right. She allowed herself to be arranged with an Indian boy, Rick Singh, whom she met through friends of our parents. The third time they saw each other, Simmi asked Rick to marry her. They were married a year later.

I had my brother's and my sister's experiences very much in mind when, after about a year and a half of playing the "he's just a friend" game with my parents, I went home from Clemson one weekend to confront them. Summoning all my courage, I sat them down and I told them: Michael's more than a friend. We're in love. I guess I knew going in what my mother's response would be, although I hoped and prayed for something different. She said bluntly that he and I could never happen. "It's just not acceptable," she told me. After that I didn't say much to my parents about Michael for a while. We continued to see each other. On the occasions he would see my parents or come up in conversation, Mom always reminded me that we could only be friends.

We dated for five years. Then, in 1994, Michael proposed to me in the botanical gardens on the Clemson campus. We both showed up at

Mom and Dad's house to tell them the news. I wasn't sure what I expected, but I know I didn't expect what they said next. Mom and Dad sat Michael down, and Dad said, "Michael, you're a good boy. If you really want to marry our daughter, you have to get a job, you have to buy a house, you have to buy a car and"—and this was what really threw us for a loop—"you can't see her or have any communication with her for a year. If you can do all these things, you can marry her." I remember feeling like I was in a movie. "You can't do this!" I sobbed to my willful parents. "This is wrong! I love him!" It was quite a scene.

When we got in the car to leave, I was very angry with my parents, but Michael was very calm. He was respectful to them, despite the outrageous conditions they had put on his proposal to me. We both wanted to do the right thing. Michael and I knew I couldn't get married without my mom and dad being there. There was no way I would be happy, and there was no way he would be happy, if our families weren't with us as we walked down the aisle. So we waited—we ignored my father's ultimatum that we not see each other for a year—but we waited. We dated for two more years. Finally I went back to my mom and dad and said, "I love him. He's very good to me. If you think you can find me someone who will love me more than him and who will take care of me better than him, then I will listen to you."

That was it for my dad. He told me he couldn't make that promise. And from that point on, they accepted Michael. We started planning a huge wedding. I was so thrilled that everyone would be there, together, that I planned five days of parties and golf tournaments and dinners for early September on Hilton Head Island, where Michael's parents live. To honor both our families' traditions, we planned an Indian service for the morning and a Christian wedding for the afternoon. It was going to be perfect.

Then, the Tuesday before my Saturday wedding, my future father-in-law called from Hilton Head. They were forecasting bad weather for the weekend, he said. Hurricane Fran was coming. But a little weather wasn't going to deter me from getting married that weekend. "So we won't play golf," I said. "What's the problem?"

"You don't understand," he said. "The caterers are leaving the island. The cake maker is leaving the island. We can't do a wedding this weekend."

I think I cried for three days. We had waited so long. I had planned such a beautiful wedding. But while I was busy feeling sorry for myself, Simmi, my mom, and Sonya got busy organizing a wedding for me in Columbia. The whole family got together to pull it off. We had an Indian service on September 7 in Columbia, and a month later we were married in a Christian ceremony at St. Andrew By-the-Sea on Hilton Head. We had our perfect wedding after all. It had been seven years and one hurricane in the making, but it was perfect because everyone we loved was there. I look back on my wedding and I am reminded of what really matters in life. I was married to the person I loved (and love!), and my family loved him too. I was a lucky and blessed girl.

Our life together was made complete in 1998 when our daughter, Rena, was born and in 2001 when our son, Nalin, came to us. All parents feel blessed, but we had difficulty having both of them, so we feel additionally blessed that God smiled on us and allowed them to be part of our lives.

The second test of my newly minted college confidence came when I entered the workforce with my new degree. Right after I graduated in 1994, I landed the kind of job most accounting majors wait years to find. It was in Charlotte with a recycling company. I was the new accounting supervisor for the company and five of its subsidiaries. I would be in charge of the accounting for all the recycling plants, closing out the books every month and producing financial statements. All of it.

I was pretty giddy when I started. I remember walking into the boardroom in our fancy corporate office the day of our first board meeting and seeing a conference table full of men. I was the first and only female executive the company had ever had, but I wasn't intimidated, only excited. The CEO was running late, so everyone was chit-chatting, waiting for the meeting to start. I sat down and exchanged pleasantries with the gray-suited man to my right. Suddenly the CEO walked in the door. Everyone grew quiet. Then one of the other executives turned to me and said, "Nikki, why don't you go get Paul a cup of coffee?"

I was stunned. I didn't know what I was going to do next, but whatever I did, I knew it would dictate how my colleagues treated me from there on out. I smiled politely and said, "Okay." Then I picked up the phone and dialed my secretary.

"Pam," I said, "would you please get Paul a cup of coffee?"

I don't know where my response came from. It was instinctive somehow. But I was right. They all looked at me, stopped talking for a second, and then went on with the meeting. From then on, my colleagues treated me as an equal. I think the executive's reasons for asking me to get coffee had as much to do with my youth as my gender. But my response seemed to overcome both of those perceived handicaps in the eyes of my colleagues. No one ever asked me to get coffee in a board meeting again.

My job involved working with each plant manager on his or her financial reporting. It was a great experience in how businesses live or die by paying attention to their bottom line, being productive, and having a motivated workforce. The goal was to run each plant processing glass, paper, and metal at its maximum capacity, operating both efficiently and safely. At the end of every month, I supervised an accounting team that had to compile all of the results of the month to tell a story of the company. Through these numbers I saw firsthand the effects that a business environment had on a plant. I remember studying other states and seeing that the challenges a plant had in Connecticut were very different from the challenges in North Carolina or Florida—all thanks to the different tax and regulatory burdens different states put on their businesses.

After working in Charlotte for a couple of years, I went back home to Bamberg to rejoin my parents' business. I had learned a lot as a corporate executive, and now I wanted to put what I had learned to work for my family business. By then the business, Exotica International, Inc., had moved eighteen miles away from Bamberg to Orangeburg. My portfolio of responsibilities, thanks to my mom, expanded considerably from when I was thirteen. Now I was doing the accounting, budgeting, and sales reports but also helping out with marketing. I watched with awe and pride as my mom's store grew to a seven-thousand-square-foot business with over a million dollars in annual sales.

Like any good small businesswoman, I joined the chamber of commerce, first in Orangeburg and then later in Lexington when we moved to a ten-thousand-square-foot store in West Columbia in 2000. I also got involved with a group called the National Association of Women Business Owners (NAWBO). This was a group of women who got together once a month to network and talk about the problems women face in the business world. There was one meeting in 2003, after I had been back in my parents' business for several years, that was pivotal. It was a particularly rancorous gathering. One after another, I watched as these small businesswomen got up and complained about this or that obstacle they were facing. The negativity bothered me. They were strong women, but they were feeling stalled by roadblocks thrown up by government.

I wasn't one to speak up much in those days. But I felt a solidarity with these women that wouldn't allow me to just sit there in silence. So I stood up. I talked about the need for self-empowerment, and I found myself echoing my parents: What we needed to do as women business owners was to stop complaining and start doing. I can't remember what they were now, but I gave some examples of possible solutions.

It was a wake-up moment for me. The women in the room actually listened. They even started taking notes! Pretty soon everyone was talking to one another about how to move forward. Something important stirred among the group that day. I might have gotten it started, but it found its strength and speed among all of us. We collectively realized that we could control our own destiny, just as my parents had when they decided to move to America. There was opportunity for us too, if we decided to take it.

I drove home that night and called my sister. "Something amazing just happened," I told her. "I moved people tonight in a way that empowered them. I need to do that for more people. I don't know how yet, but I have to figure out a way to get people to understand the power of their own voice."

After my epiphany at the women's meeting, I started talking to friends about ways I could make a difference. Then, at a NAWBO meeting shortly after the one in which I spoke up, I met a woman named Eleanor Kitzman and we started talking about empowering women and their role in politics. We became immediate friends. Eleanor was a successful businesswoman and CEO of Drivers Choice Insurance. I will always be grateful to her because she was the first in a series of women who believed in what I could be. She and I both believed in giving back in a way that empowered others—in paying it forward. She asked me if I had ever thought about getting involved in politics. I said no, I hadn't. And it was true. I didn't even know where to start.

What I did know was what I had lived and experienced, and that was business. It is business—particularly small business—that is at the heart of any economy, and yet government always seems to throw the most burdens on it. How could I get government to realize that business owners were the group you never touched, the group that needed the most freedom to grow and expand? If you take care of your businesses, you take care of the economy, education, and quality of life for everyone.

The first thing Eleanor did was take me to lunch and start asking me questions.

"Are you a Republican or a Democrat?" she asked.

"I don't know," I said.

"So what do you believe?"

I told her I believed in protecting the rights and freedom of the people. I believed in the amazing survival skills of small businesses. I believed that everyone should live within their means and that government shouldn't be exempt from that. Parties were labels I didn't care about, I told her. They clouded arguments and kept people from thinking for themselves.

"Oh, you are clearly a Republican," Eleanor said when I finished.

Eleanor suggested I meet with Rita Allison, who had previously been a member of the state house and had run unsuccessfully for lieutenant governor. Now she worked in higher education for Governor Mark Sanford. I met with Rita and we talked for a while about political opportunities. I told her that everyone was telling me I needed to start small, with the school board. Miss Rita disagreed. "Have you looked at your house district?" she asked.

I said no.

"Do you even know who your house member is?"

No.

"I think it's Larry Koon, and I hear he may be retiring," she said. "You should look at that district."

Encouraged, I went and checked. Lo and behold, I did live in Representative Koon's district. It was a staunchly conservative district that encompassed Lexington County, just outside Columbia. If you won the Republican primary, you won the seat. Mr. Koon had represented the 87th District for thirty years, longer than any other member of the state legislature. But just as Miss Rita had said, he was hinting that he might retire that year.

I thought about it. No one knew who I was. I had no name recognition. I wasn't "from there." The list of reasons why I shouldn't do it went on and on. But still, I thought . . . *I could do this.* My parents had always refused to let all the reasons I had to be insecure—all the differences I had from those around me—define me. They made me push myself into challenges that were uncomfortable so that I would gain the confidence to get past those challenges. All of it could have made me more insecure, but instead it had made me stronger. This was another challenge. And I knew that if the voters of the 87th District gave me a chance, I would spend my entire term trying to prove to them that they had made the right decision.

Michael and I laugh about it now. Somewhere along the line, I internalized that need to push through challenges to the degree that I constantly box myself into corners by making commitments that then challenge me to honor them. I'll say something definitive about how I'm going to do this or that, or how something I'm doing is going to be the biggest and best ever, and in the back of my mind I'm thinking, "*Now, how am I going to pull this off?*" More than once I have been blessed by the truism that ignorance is bliss. Sometimes God smiles and says, "You just don't need to know what's ahead of you." At no point in my life has this been more true than that day talking to Miss Rita. The pain of that first house race is one I wouldn't wish on anyone. But I didn't know that at the time, so I said, "Okay, let's do it."

I had committed myself. I was running for the legislature. There was no turning back. The only option was to win.

Chapter Three
Nikki Who?

I was an announced candidate for the 87th District of the South Carolina House of Representatives when I found out that the incumbent wasn't retiring after all. Not only that, but he was related to half the district. No fooling. Half the district. And the half that wasn't a part of Representative Larry Koon's family was a part of another old South Carolina family, the Rawls. Both families traced their roots in South Carolina back to the 1700s. Upon realizing this, I put my head in my hands and said to Michael: "What have I done?"

When I started going around telling people I was running for the state house, I got a lot of responses. Some people looked at me like they felt sorry for me. Others suggested, yet again, that I not set my sights so high. Perhaps I would be more comfortable running for the school board? My parents and Michael were the only ones who were with me. They kept reminding me that there wasn't anything I couldn't do. My mom told me again what she had said to me many times: If you do something, be great at it. Let people remember you were here.

Michael and I began doing our homework. We sought out the advice of yet another wise woman, Deb Sofield. Deb had run for comptroller general a few years before and lost. But she knew the rules of the road, and I was in desperate need of a navigator. So she and I, along with Eleanor and Rita, decamped to a restaurant to begin my tutoring. Looking back, I realize that this group of savvy women must have seen how naive I was. Deb in particular put up with a lot. "Nikki, you have to go to Republican meetings," was one of her first pieces of advice. I remember asking her, "What do I wear?" Deb is tough and always gave me my medicine when I needed it. "Really, Nikki, boy, do we have a lot of work to do with you," she said. Still, the notion that I *not* run never entered the conversation. These ladies patiently and wisely answered my questions and gave me good advice. I will always be grateful to the women—and strangely, it was mostly women—who told me to go for it and then showed me how.

Deb's second piece of advice was that I get a political consultant. Now, if you ask me, the consultants' side of politics in South Carolina is a warped one. They are part of what I believe is the negative side of public service. Too often consultants care about winning at almost any cost and have little imagination for any candidate who does not meet their preconceived ideas about who can win.

My case in point is the first consultant who was recommended to us. I called him and was completely unprepared for the conversation that took place. "What's your background?" he asked. I told him I was Indian. "There's not many Indians in Lexington County. Are you prolife or prochoice? Do your parents attend that Indian church?" "That Indian church"? What did that mean? The stupid questions went on and on until I finally got fed up. I told him I just wanted to run for office.

"I know who I am," I said, exasperated. "I know what I can do. I just want the chance to do it."

And that's when I got my reality check. "I'm going to be straight with you," he said. "You're attractive, but you're an Indian woman. You're only thirty-one years old. Your dad wears a headdress. Lexington County is just not going to support that."

I guess I couldn't take a hint. "So does that mean you won't help me?" I replied.

Michael and I had a breakfast meeting with the second consultant. It was a great meeting. He liked what I had to say. I convinced him that I would work hard and raise money. Michael and I left the meeting high-fiving. I'd finally gotten my consultant! He would get us a proposal and we would go forward. The whole thing was beginning to feel real.

Then a day went by, and another. No word from the consultant. I left messages. Michael e-mailed him. Finally, three days later, he called. "I'm sorry, I just can't take your race," he said. I told him I didn't understand. He said it was not in his best interest to take it. With Mr. Koon staying in the race and defending his seat, he didn't feel like it was a race that could be won—by me, that is.

We tried a third consultant. Same thing.

I finally called Deb.

"Deb, no one will take my money."

In my experience, if you have the money to pay someone to do a job for you, they will generally do it. My parents had loaned me some money to get my campaign started, but no one would take it. Deb was frustrated too. It's unusual for consultants not to take money, even if it is a race they aren't sure they can win. True, I was going up against the longest-serving member of the house, but still. I wondered if there was more going on. It was a low point for me. I had found what I believed was a chance to make a difference in people's lives, and no one other than my family believed I could do it.

Deb spoke with Michael, and they decided we might just have to run the race ourselves. She believed it was important that we get a good walking and mailing list of voters to work from. One day she sent a kid over who was supposed to be great at lists and targeting them toward solid primary voters. It was a Sunday. I was under a blanket in sweatpants on the couch, wallowing in self-pity. The kid showed up and I barely said two words to him. Instead, Michael talked to him. I remember asking Michael after he left, "Why bother?" He told me— not for the first or the last time—not to give up. We would find a way. I still wasn't sure.

Deb called that night. "I have an idea," she said. "Why don't you hire that kid?" I remember saying, "Deb, you can't be serious." She quickly put me in my place. "It's not like you have people knocking on your door to help," she said.

The kid's name was B. J. Boling. When I finally came to my senses, I hired him. He was looking to prove himself, and I was a candidate who was determined to win. It was a perfect fit. Through our mutual hunger, that first Haley campaign was born. He killed himself for the campaign. He put his heart and soul into it. He knew it was an uphill battle, but he also knew that with my work ethic and his knowledge and passion, we could win. In the end, he believed in me and I believed in him.

I will forever be thankful that we both trusted enough to give each other a chance.

With Mr. Koon staying in, it was a three-way race for the Republican nomination. Besides the incumbent and me, another political first-timer, insurance agent David Perry, chairman of the Lexington Chamber of Commerce, had entered the race. From the start, no one took me very seriously. I was discounted because I was a girl. I was discounted because I was Indian. I was discounted because I was young. Looking back, it's hard to blame people. It was a David-versus-Goliath race. Residents of the district had been voting for Mr. Koon for thirty years. To them, I was "Nikki who?" It became a running joke in later campaigns. I always started out as Nikki Who.

Still, I was determined. Losing was not an option. My strategy was simple: I would grab a box of Krispy Kremes and a bunch of coffees and go from neighborhood to neighborhood, knocking on doors. Michael would drive me with the kids in the backseat. I just showed up and said, "Hi, I'm Nikki Haley and I'm running for the state house, and I'd appreciate your vote." We went wherever we could. There wasn't a day in the entire campaign that I didn't knock on doors, either after work or on Saturday and Sunday afternoons.

We did everything we were supposed to do. We had signs everywhere. What little money I had I put toward sending mailers to voters in the district. I was always careful to make them about me and not about my opponents. I promised to bring my small-business common sense to government. I promised to make government work for the people again. I spoke respectfully about Mr. Koon, saying I appreciated his service but that it was time for something different in the state house. Someone who was going to fight for the residents of the district. Someone who would bring a new approach.

We didn't have the money to do any polling, so about a week before the primary I called a friend who worked in the state senate and asked her what the numbers looked like. If no candidate in the primary got more than 50 percent of the vote, there would be a runoff to determine the nominee. I didn't have the confidence to think I could avoid the runoff, but I thought I had a shot at being one of the two candidates who made it to the deciding contest. My friend called me back a few hours later and said, "I just don't want to tell you this." I asked her what she didn't want to tell me. "You have fifteen percent," she said.

I was astonished. It was a week before the primary. We had worked so hard and knocked on so many doors. And for what? For 15 percent?

And then, a few days later, with the primary just days away, the other shoe dropped. I started to get calls from supporters in the district. People were receiving a mailer saying Governor Mark Sanford was endorsing Mr. Koon. It didn't make sense to me. Mr. Koon was an old-school member of the legislature, a reliable vote for the status quo who didn't rock the boat. Governor Sanford, in contrast, was a reformer who was taking on business as usual in the statehouse. It just didn't make sense that the governor would make an endorsement in the GOP primary, and if he did, that he would throw his considerable political weight behind Larry Koon.

We called the governor's office to see if they had, in fact, sent out the mailer. Sure enough, they told us they had not. They hadn't endorsed anybody. But the primary was just days away, and the lie was out there. B.J. asked if they would write a letter saying Governor Sanford hadn't endorsed Mr. Koon. Sanford's office agreed to write a letter saying he didn't endorse candidates in primaries. Good enough, I thought. But there was so little time. When we got the letter, Michael and our neighbor down the street, Paul Ifkovits, who owned a bulk-mail business, went to work. They worked all night, printing, folding, and stapling our mailer. It had Mr. Koon's dishonest flier on one side and Governor Sanford's letter on the other. It was a simple, uncomplicated message to the voters that they had been duped. It dropped the day of the election.

There was another piece of mail that last week that helped turn the tide for us. We had a friend, John Barefoot, who was Googling around trying to find out as much about Mr. Koon as he could to help out with the campaign. He came upon a book called *The Stupidest Things Ever Said by Politicians*. There, on page thirty-eight, was this:

"Women are best suited for secretarial work, decorating cakes and counter sales, like selling lingerie."

—South Carolina state representative Larry Koon

(R, Lexington)

John took the quote to my women's business group, NAWBO, and the group didn't hesitate. It reprinted Mr. Koon's statement on a black background in archaic-looking script and put it out. The women of the district were furious. On election day, the vote was Perry 17 percent, Haley 40 percent, and Koon 42 percent. We had made it to the runoff.

If I thought the three-way primary was tough, I had no idea what I was getting into going head-to-head against the forces of the status quo in South Carolina's 87th District. The runoff was a two-week sprint, and the Koon campaign didn't waste any time before it started trying to paint me as the outsider in my own community.

One day Michael and I were stuffing HALEY FOR STATE HOUSE fliers into newspaper boxes when we saw a car up ahead of us also clearly putting something into the boxes. I grabbed one of the fliers out of a paper box and looked. It was a side-by-side comparison card with Larry Koon's picture on one side and mine on the other. Under Mr. Koon's picture it said "white male," under mine, "Indian female." On his side, "Christian." On mine (incorrectly), "Buddhist." Under his picture, "business owner." Under mine, "housekeeper." And on and on. Every description was designed to either demean me or portray me as different from the voters.

I decided to confront the man distributing the card. Michael drove up to the man and blocked him in with the car. I got out. "What are you doing?" I asked.

"The same thing you are."

"No," I said. "I'm talking about me. You're spreading lies."

"Ma'am," he said, "I'm just doing my job. We don't think you're right for this district."

The card was the beginning of a whisper campaign that I wasn't a Christian. When I look back on it, this was among the most painful periods of that campaign or any campaign I've run. The rumors flying around forced me for the first time to talk publicly about the issue of religion in my life.

I suppose my religious experiences are a bit more complicated than those of most politicians, but my story is really pretty simple.

I am proud of the spiritual way my parents raised me. I grew up in a family full of faith. My parents spoke to us about religion a lot. And they taught us by example: Faith and respect went hand in hand; turning the other cheek and treating people with compassion were daily activities. I never knew a time—even in the most challenging of financial circumstances—when my mom and dad weren't giving their time to some charity or helping some organization that was giving to those less fortunate.

Because there was, and still is, such a small Indian community in South Carolina, and an even smaller Sikh community, when I was growing up a handful of families would get together randomly at someone's home to worship. These services were three-day-long rituals of prayer followed by copious amounts of wonderful food, and they usually took place about once a month. The Sikhs I grew up with are a very thoughtful, graceful group who understand that the best way to appreciate God's blessings is to give back. Doing for others is their way to God. You always felt God in the room during those services. Many of those who attended were educated, wealthy, and successful, but all of these accomplishments were always left at the door, as everyone understood they would never have been possible without the involvement of God's hands. To them, humility was more important than any amount of wealth or success.

Although I will always respect and be grateful for the faith in which I was raised, I eventually strayed and found the religious home that truly spoke to me.

When Michael and I were dating, we had many heartfelt conversations about religion. Those talks touched a lot on the circumstances of his birth, savior, and upbringing. And they touched on our mutual desire to bring God into our lives in a more personal and direct way than I had growing up. When I attended Sikh worship services as a young person, I gained an appreciation for God's presence, but because the ceremony was conducted in Punjabi, I never truly understood the message. As much as my parents wanted us to learn Punjabi, I was too preoccupied to focus on it. Faith became something I developed without actually understanding scripture. I converted to Christianity because the teachings of Christ spoke to me in a way that I could understand and that would help me live my life—the life I wanted in mine and Michael's marriage and in the raising of our children.

To me this was all very personal. As a newcomer to politics, it came as quite a shock to me that my faith journey was something that would be dissected by political opponents on the campaign trail. It's not that I was uncomfortable talking about being Christian. I wasn't. Michael and I were married in the Christian faith. Our children were baptized as Christians. We attend church regularly. It was and is central to our lives. It was just that I never wanted to hurt my parents' feelings. I never wanted my parents to see this as something I thought they did wrong in raising me.

That idea—that my parents had done something wrong by raising me the way they did—was exactly what my opponents wanted voters to believe. They would not be satisfied unless I said my parents were going to hell and the way they lived their life was wrong. I wasn't about to do that then, and I never will.

I tried my best to answer people's questions about this deeply personal issue in the state house race. When I ran for governor, critics tried again to use religion against me. My response was to open all of my speeches with this simple assertion: "I am the proud daughter of Indian parents who reminded me every day how blessed I was to live in this country." For a few people that wasn't enough. But most South Carolinians respect the decisions Michael and I have made in our walk with the Lord.

My conversion and my walk with God as a Christian remain intensely personal to me. I will probably never be one of those politicians who sprinkles biblical passages into every speech. Mind you, I have no objection to those who do. The effort by some in our country to remove religion from public discourse is entirely wrong. Public policy would benefit from more, not less, infusion of religious values. But I think maybe my upbringing as a religious minority has made me sensitive to how religious talk can easily become politically manipulative. And that's just not who I am. What I do know is that you can never have too much of God in your life, and I am mindful of that every day.

Maybe it's because I have so much religion in my life, but I truly believe in signs from God. One night during the worst part of the state house race, when I was getting no traction and felt like I wasn't being accepted, we had dinner at a Chinese restaurant. As hokey as it sounds, I found a message in a fortune cookie that guided me for the rest of the race:

Winners do what losers don't want to.

I taped the fortune to my computer so I would never forget it: I was the underdog. I needed to do what my opponent didn't want to. In elections, candidates usually go where they know their support is. I made the conscious decision to go where I knew my support was *not*. I went to places that were uncomfortable. I went to a biker bar. I remember shaking all these guys' hands and answering their questions about motorcycle rights and gun rights. Before I knew it, they were fighting for me and telling their friends to support me.

When I speak to groups of young people today, I always tell them they need to have three war stories—three stories in which they did something that was uncomfortable and came out stronger for it. If you don't have three war stories, I tell them, you have more living to do and you need to challenge yourself. If they do have three war stories, I congratulate them and encourage them to keep doing what they're doing.

Most people can't think of three stories in which they truly challenged themselves. But when you go where you're uncomfortable, when you do what others won't do, you usually find strength you didn't know you had. This was my story, over and over, growing up and throughout that first state house campaign. I couldn't stand the thought that there were people out there who didn't know me and didn't support me. I believed that if they got a chance to meet me, I could bring them around. In any case, doing nothing was never an option. I had to try. I had to do something. If they ended up not supporting me, then so be it. But I couldn't let them make that decision without first knowing me.

My first war story came early in the campaign, when I was still working on answering the "Nikki who?" question and trying to get people to know who I was. I got a call one day from a man I didn't know personally but who I knew was a businessman and a potential donor. He said he wanted to meet with me, and I enthusiastically accepted. When I went to his office for the meeting, he took me into a boardroom with seven or eight other men seated around the table. I hadn't expected to meet with a group, but no matter. I sat down at the head of the table and launched into my sell about encouraging business and economic development by lowering taxes and getting government out of the way. They let me go on, and when I was finished the businessman said, "Look, you're young. And it's obvious you're a smart girl. But we have a friend who wants to run in this race. If you step out, we'll make sure you get a good position—a good appointment—when he wins."

It was another of those moments of absolute panic, like that day in the boardroom when I was asked to get coffee. I didn't know how to respond, but I knew what I said would matter.

"You are so kind. Thank you very much," I found myself saying. "But you know what? I already raised twenty-five thousand dollars, and I'm going to double it by next month. And I'm going to win this race. But I tell you what. Why don't you go tell your friend that if he decides to step out of this race, I'd be happy to consider him for a position or an appointment."

I remember getting in the car after the meeting, out of breath, calling Michael to tell him what had happened. I had been ambushed, I told him. I didn't know what to do, so I decided to make an opportunity out of the situation. The group of men tried to push me, and I pushed back. Somehow, I showed them that I had some courage and some fight in me. And that, it turned out, was what they had been looking for all along.

"So what happened?" he said. "How did you end it?"

"I got a thousand dollars out of every one of them," I said.

Later in the campaign I discovered something about myself when, again, I went somewhere uncomfortable. Every year Ducks Unlimited, a group dedicated to conserving wetlands for waterfowl, has a fund-raiser in Lexington County. It's a big social event that always attracts hundreds of the county's most well-heeled residents. When the event came around during the state house campaign, I decided to go to see if I could shake a few hands and win a few votes. As usual, I dragged Michael along. I remember walking into this huge room, with my HALEY FOR HOUSE badge on, and knowing very few people there—except for Mr. Koon, who was standing with a long line of people waiting to talk to him.

I made a point, at every event during the campaign that we both attended, to greet Mr. Koon and shake his hand before I talked to anyone else. I thought it was the respectful thing to do. So I got in line at the Ducks Unlimited event to shake his hand. And as I got closer, I saw a man get up on the stage and start to speak.

"I want y'all to know that Larry Koon is in the house tonight," the man said to the crowd. "He *is* running. I'm going to support him and I want everyone in this room to support him."

Just as I stepped up to Mr. Koon to shake his hand, the room broke out in thunderous applause. Mr. Koon looked at me and said, "See, little lady. These people love me." I said, "Yes, sir, they do."

All I could think of was how unwelcome I was in that room. All I could think of was how badly I wanted to leave—and if I felt that way, I knew Michael felt the same way times two. But I didn't leave. *Winners do what losers don't want to.* I remember forcing myself to work the room that night. God bless Michael for staying with me as I walked around, saying hello and shaking hands. It was one of the hardest things I had to do throughout the whole campaign, holding my head up, surrounded by all these people who'd just heard what the man had said. But I knew I had to do something. I couldn't just run away and let him win.

I found out later that the man on the stage was Larry Koon's cousin. So about three weeks later, I drove out to his business. I didn't really think about it; I just did it. *I had to do something.* Somehow I got him to come out of his office to see me. I said, "Hey, I'm Nikki Haley."

And he said he knew who I was. And I asked him if I could talk to him for a few minutes. We went into his office and I started to launch into my campaign pitch. He interrupted me after a few seconds.

"I don't mean to be rude," he said, "but why are you here? I just stood up in front of a thousand people and told them I was supporting my cousin."

"I want you to know who I am and I want you to know why I'm running," I said. "And when you're at home or you're with your friends, in those quiet circles, I want you to tell them you liked what I had to say."

He looked at me like I was nuts. "You want me to what?" he said.

"Nobody knows who you vote for behind that curtain. I'm not asking you to put a sign in your yard or in front of your business," I said. "I just want you to tell your friends how great I was."

He sat there for a second. Eventually he said, "Okay, thanks for stopping by."

"My pleasure," I said. "There's just one more thing before I leave. I need a thousand-dollar check."

Maybe he agreed with me; maybe he just wanted to get rid of me. But he gave me the check. It was the best feeling. I had challenged myself and come away the better for it. I told myself I did it for the campaign, but looking back I can see I really did it for me. I did it so I could go to sleep that night knowing I was stronger than I had been the day before.

I slept like a baby that night.

My third war story from the state house campaign involves yet another Koon cousin, this one the most powerful and influential of them all. He had a massive farm located on a well-traveled stretch of road in Lexington County. I met him at a restaurant one day, and I told him his support was important to me. He told me the usual: "You realize Larry is my cousin, don't you?" I told him I did. I said I wasn't asking him to put up a sign or anything. I just wanted him to tell people he had met me and liked what I had to say. I knew his word carried a lot of weight in the district. If I could get that much out of him, it would help my campaign.

After our initial meeting I would see him at events and always make a habit of going over to speak to him. He never said much to me. But occasionally he gave me a sign I was breaking through. Sometimes, instead of my coming up to him, he came over to me to say hello. I started to have some hope.

Then one day I was driving around with Michael (the kids had wised up and would no longer sit in the backseat, so they were home with Mom and Dad), and we went by the cousin's house. I looked, and there was a Larry Koon sign in his front yard. It was two weeks before the election. I was genuinely dejected. "Michael, I have tried so hard with him," I said. "Putting up that sign is telling the whole community who to vote for. I can't believe he's doing this." Michael told me (not for the first or the last time) to let it go.

The next week we drove by and lo and behold, there was a HALEY FOR STATE HOUSE sign right next to the Koon sign! I thought it was the coolest thing. "He's telling people to vote their conscience," I told Michael. "He's telling everybody it's okay!" There was still hope.

And then, a week before the runoff, we rode by the cousin's house. The Larry Koon sign was gone. There, standing alone in his front yard, was a HALEY FOR STATE HOUSE sign. It was his way of telling everyone this was whom they should support. I thought about my fortune cookie. *Winners do what losers don't want to.* I had certainly done a lot of things I wasn't particularly thrilled to do. Maybe it would all be worth it.

Despite these hard-earned successes, toward the end of the state house campaign, things got truly ugly. A half-page ad appeared in the local Lexington newspaper proclaiming that "there is only one REAL Republican in the run-off." It went on to say that Mr. Koon had voted in every recent Republican primary, whereas "Nimrata N. Randhawa" had once voted in a Democratic primary. "Nimrata" is my given name, but I have spent my whole life as Nikki. Some have accused me of creating the name "Nikki" to sound American, but on my birth certificate it says, "Nimrata Nikki Randhawa." And of course, now that I was married, my last name was Haley. But never mind. The message of the ad was clear: She's not one of us.

Then Michael and I started to get hate calls at our home. To make matters worse, somehow my cell-phone number got out and people began to call me and scream into the phone. No words, just screams. The calls came constantly, day and night. It got so bad that I couldn't answer my own phone. Then I started to be followed in my car. One day I actually had to pull into a police station to lose a truck that had been tailing me. And scariest of all, strangers started to drive by our house very slowly. They would cruise by, then turn around and ride by again. Michael and I agreed we could no longer let the kids play outside.

It was emotional and mental abuse, and it began to take its toll. I'm five feet six inches tall, and I normally keep to a healthy weight. But by the end of that campaign, I was down to less than a hundred pounds. I remember going to Michael one day in tears and telling him that I couldn't keep anything down. My parents were very concerned. Dad finally went out and bought me a bunch of those nutrition shakes. I lived on those for the rest of the campaign.

Amazingly, the harassment continued, even on the day of the run-off. All over the district my volunteers were going home crying and upset. One woman holding a HALEY FOR STATE HOUSE sign outside a polling place stood in confusion as a man driving past rolled down his window and shouted, "I hope your children worship cows!" We decided later that this misinformed person thought I was Hindu and meant his comment to be a put-down of Hindus. I couldn't believe it was still going on. The volunteer told me she yelled back, "They're more American than you could ever dream of being!" My volunteers were (and are!) the best.

I decided to spend election day at Mr. Koon's voting precinct to catch any last-minute deciders. At some point during the day, Mr. Koon also showed up. He came over to me, surrounded by an entourage of his four grown sons, and said, "You know, little lady"—he liked to call me "little lady"—"this is the first time in thirty years I've had to stand at a poll." Maybe he knew something I didn't. I honestly didn't know who was going to win. All I knew was that I had worked hard—my body and my mind were more tired than they had ever been before. I told Mr. Koon it had been a pleasure to compete against him. And then I began to notice something. A steady stream of voters was coming in. I watched as they all came and shook Mr. Koon's hand and said hello. They all clearly knew him. But as they walked by me, more often than not, they would wink and smile. They were telling me that they couldn't say so openly, but they were voting for me. It was then that I knew we had it.

Election night was a blur. I met Mom, Dad, Michael, and the kids at a restaurant for a small election-night party, but I still couldn't eat. When the returns came in, I had defeated Mr. Koon 55 percent to 45 percent. I was in shock. An era had truly ended in the 87th District. I had unseated the longest-serving member of the state house. A reporter came up to me and asked me what I had to say. I said I had big shoes to fill and my goal now was to make Mr. Koon proud. I was genuinely humbled to win. Mr. Koon never called to congratulate me that night. To this day, he has never spoken another word to me.

I woke up the morning after the runoff with one thought going through my head: *We won! Now what?* As I lay there in bed, still exhausted, Michael brought me the newspaper. I turned to the story on the state house race, looked up at Michael, and said, "Am I reading this right?" The story included my quote about making Mr. Koon proud and mentioned that I hoped to call on him for advice. It was his quote in response that caused my disbelief.

"I have very little reason to offer anything to her," the story reported Mr. Koon saying. "I really think they [the voters] don't know what they got."

I was speechless. I had always tried to be respectful. But I wasn't the only one who noticed Mr. Koon's comment. I smiled a few days later when I read a letter in the newspaper from a reader who was also outraged by Mr. Koon's quote. Playing off his comment that the voters "don't know what they got," the person wrote, "Well, they were intelligent enough to know that they didn't want what they had."

Even after they lost the primary, the forces of the establishment in the 87th District didn't give up. I got a call a few weeks later from a woman I didn't know telling me that someone had just been to her house collecting signatures for a candidate to run against me in the general election. So-called petition candidates very rarely succeed, and this person was no exception. When the elections commission went through the signatures he had collected, they found fictitious and dead people's names. When they threw out his candidacy, we were finally able to breathe a sign of relief.

Mr. Koon and his campaign always maintained that they knew nothing about the harassment and abuse my family and I endured during the campaign. But the heartening thing for me was that the people of South Carolina rose above it. They were sick of the kind of politics that had given our state a bad name. The campaign against me had crossed a line. It didn't matter if you were a Republican or a Democrat; Christian, Hindu, or Sikh; or white, black, or brown. It was ugly, and people were tired of the ugliness.

Some might be tempted to use the story of my state house race as yet another example of what's wrong with South Carolina. But just like the story of my childhood in Bamberg, the story of that state house race is ultimately defined not by its details but by its ending. An editorial writer for the *State*, one of South Carolina's largest newspapers, wrote a postmortem of the race that summed it up well. Under the headline "Voters Embraced American Dream in Choosing Nikki Haley," Warthen wrote that the real story of the race wasn't the ugly tactics it featured against me. "The real story is that the people of House District 87 rose above the whispered nonsense and chose her over the man who had represented them for the past 30 years."

The article concluded with a quote from the volunteer who had been heckled carrying the HALEY FOR STATE HOUSE sign on election day. I don't know if I've ever been prouder to be a South Carolinian and to be an American than when I read her words.

"Isn't it something," she said, "that a person whose parents are from another country can portray America better than you and I can? They can teach us a lesson of what it means to be an American."

That's what I've tried to do every day since.

Chapter Four
The Good Old Boys' Club

Legislatures—and the South Carolina legislature is no exception—are clubs. They have rules. Play by the rules and you remain a member in good standing. Break the rules and, well, you can get locked out of the clubhouse.

I came to the South Carolina house in 2005 having already broken a rule. I had unseated the longest-serving legislator in South Carolina history—a real good old boy. Luckily, I had company. Nathan Ballentine, a banker with roots so deep in South Carolina that the community he comes from is called Ballentine, had also broken the club rules to get in. He had unseated the majority leader. Nathan and I were the skunks at the garden party. No one wanted to be near us. So we became friends by default. Later we would become genuine friends through our shared commitment to shaking up politics as usual in Columbia. But in the beginning, we came together as outsiders. No one wanted to share a desk with us, so we became seatmates in the house chamber. No one wanted to share an office with us, so we shared a suite in the legislative office building.

For Nathan and me the first day at the statehouse was like our first day of school. At the meeting of the Republican caucus, the incumbents patted one another on the back like old friends, while we stood off to the side, not sure what to do. We had defeated their friends, and we were feeling it. We knew it would take time for them to get to know us and for us to prove ourselves.

I remember standing in the caucus room waiting for the meeting to start. Lobbyists, reporters, and legislators were buzzing all around. One legislator who had been nice to me by stopping by my office to visit after I had won the election—one of the few members I actually knew—came up to me. He said he wanted to ask me a question. From time to time, companies will sponsor lunches for the Republican house members, he said, and they cater all kinds of things. Then he started to mumble and look nervous. "Well, you know . . . sometimes they have barbecue, sometimes chicken. . . . Um, well, we were wondering if there were certain things that you may not eat."

I got his point. Even at thirty-two years old, I was still having to prove that I was the same as the other kids. "I can eat a hamburger with the best of them," I replied.

He rambled on for a little while and said, "Well, we weren't sure, so . . ." I stopped him and smiled. "No worries," I said. "I don't have horns either." We laughed uncomfortably. I knew his heart was in the right place. He was asking in the only way he knew how. And I was doing what I had always done when I was a kid. Trying to prove myself by finding similarities and avoiding differences. Something told me, though, that this playground would be tougher than the one back at Bamberg Elementary School.

He became known to the country for his infamous nonwalk on the Appalachian Trail, but at the time I entered the legislature, Governor Mark Sanford was leading something of a revolution in South Carolina. For generations, a good old boy system had run Columbia. It wasn't so much Democrat-versus-Republican politics in the legislature as it was go-along-to-get-along politics. Legislators supported other members' pork projects, secure in the knowledge that their colleagues would return the favor when it was their turn at the trough. The result was that first Democrats and later Republicans created and nurtured a bloated, inefficient state government.

Governor Sanford attacked the good old boy system head on. He consistently vetoed legislators' overspending and pork projects, and they hated him for it. He would send down budget vetoes and the GOP-led legislature would summarily override them. The year before I came to the house, in 2004, Governor Sanford issued 106 budget vetoes. The legislature took just ninety minutes to override 105 of them. In what was meant to be a lighthearted protest, Sanford showed up at the statehouse the next day with two squealing pigs, named "Pork" and "Barrel," under each arm. The members did not appreciate the joke.

What Governor Sanford called his "philosophical jihad" against bloated government continued when I came to the state house. He issued 163 vetoes that session. The story being told around Columbia was about a Republican state senator who supposedly said the following while offering a blessing: "Lord, please bless this food and help us override all these dadburned vetoes." Nathan and I did nothing to endear ourselves to our new colleagues by voting to sustain Governor Sanford's vetoes. We were fiscal conservatives. We had campaigned as fiscal conservatives, we had won as fiscal conservatives, and we intended to vote like fiscal conservatives. But we soon found out we were breaking the rules again. "That's not how we do things around here," one longtime member growled at me after I voted to sustain a veto. Things got worse for Nathan and me after those votes. I remember sitting together eating lunch with the Republican caucus and watching as the other legislators walked by, not wanting to sit next to us unless there was no other possible option. This wasn't like high school, we joked. This was like middle school. We were definitely not the cool kids.

Despite my multiple violations of the club rules, I rose quickly in the leadership in the house. My first year, my colleagues voted me chairman of the freshman class. My second year I was named majority whip—one of the members who counts the votes and works the floor to persuade other legislators on votes. In the South Carolina legislature the house speaker is very powerful. He (it's always been a "he") makes all the committee assignments. And at first, the speaker took kind of a shine to me. My third year in the house he appointed me to the powerful Labor, Commerce and Industry Committee, which I loved because it was a place where I could continue to fight to create a better environment for jobs and business in South Carolina. By my fourth year, I had been made chairman of the House Subcommittee on Banking and Consumer Affairs. I had managed to get the leadership to overlook my political heresy by working hard and indulging my passion for policy. The speaker used to joke that I would be speaker myself one day.

Things were going well for me in the legislature, but after a while I began to notice something that unsettled me. I began to see many of the members I had been elected with start to change. They stopped standing up for the things they used to believe in. They started making excuses to justify votes they knew weren't right. They started to base their friendships in the house on political back-scratching rather than shared principles. They were starting to bend to the rules of the club. One night I went home to Michael and told him, "If you ever see me doing that, tell me, because I'm afraid I won't see it." I knew my colleagues weren't seeing what was happening to them. They had gone to the state house with the best of intentions, but Columbia was changing them. They were frogs in a pot of water heading for a boil, and they couldn't feel the temperature rising.

One of the worst parts of the political culture in the legislature was the practice of not voting on the record when important pieces of legislation came up. Instead of calling the roll and recording each member's vote, the vast majority of the time the house and senate would pass bills by voice vote. That meant legislators would simply shout their votes, in unison when the clerk called for the yeas and nays. The louder voices prevailed, and no one ever went on the record. The taxpayers had no way of knowing who voted for what. Most of the voters weren't even aware this was happening, but it was a fundamental violation of what we were supposed to be doing, which was representing the people. How could the voters judge us without knowing how we voted? How could we spend the taxpayers' money without being accountable for our choices?

The more I looked into it, the more outrageous the lack of transparency in the legislature was to me. South Carolina ranked dead last in the country in terms of the voters' being able to know how their representatives voted. Unlike most states, it had no constitutional or statutory requirement that legislation be passed with a roll-call vote. And even among those states that didn't constitutionally or statutorily require on-the-record voting, South Carolina had the most difficult procedure for a legislator to request a recorded vote. In the house you had to get nine other members to join you in a call for a recorded vote. In practice, of course, that meant that any vote the leadership wanted to keep secret was kept secret, and major pieces of legislation that involved spending were being passed this way. The creation of whole new government agencies, tax exemptions, regulations on building and business—all of it was becoming law without any accountability on the part of lawmakers. State senator Jake Knotts captured the arrogance behind the ten-member requirement for a roll-call vote perfectly when he said smugly to Nathan and me, "If you don't have nine friends, you shouldn't be here."

The final straw for me came in 2008 when I watched as the members of the house voted themselves a retirement pay increase by a voice vote. The clerk called for a vote, the members shouted their votes, and the bill was declared passed. To this day, you can't find a single legislator who will say he or she voted for the bill. I was mortified. I was actually embarrassed for the house and for my colleagues. How could we allow this to happen? I went up to the speaker, clearly upset. "We're Republicans!" I said to him. "We're supposed to be for *less* spending. I can't believe you just allowed that!" I was really worked up. The speaker was too. He got red in the face and walked away. I didn't care. It was wrong and it had to stop.

It was at that point that I discovered my mission for my tenure in the South Carolina legislature: making it possible for the voters to know how their legislators voted. The current system was a violation of every notion of accountability I had ever known. In business, no sane entrepreneur would just hand over his or her checkbook to some stranger and say, "Here, spend it wisely; I don't need to know how." In the real world, people have to be responsible for how they act and how they spend. In government, it seemed to me, our obligation was even greater. We were spending the citizens' money, after all. We owed them the right to know how we were governing, and we owed ourselves the opportunity to prove to our constituents that we were trying to be more efficient and effective with their tax dollars.

That spring I got busy working on a bill that would require a roll-call vote on any legislation that had a fiscal impact—that is, any bill that spent or raised any of the taxpayers' money. I started calling around and letting my fellow members know that I would be introducing the bill in the new session the following year. It was a lonely crusade. My only ally in the legislature was Nathan.

Over the summer, the Republicans would traditionally meet at a caucus retreat to discuss the agenda for the following year. That summer when we met, I raised my hand to speak. The speaker knew what I was going to say because I had called all the leadership and left messages telling them about my plans to introduce a bill to require votes on the record. Everyone had called me back except the speaker. He didn't like my idea, and he was ready for me. In front of the entire caucus, he attacked me for daring to challenge the rules of the club. It was clear he took my proposal as a personal challenge of him, and he responded in kind. He humiliated me in front of my colleagues. I was furious. Nathan was quietly urging me to "just let it go," but I couldn't.

"How do you send people out of this room and expect them to tell their constituents that they don't deserve to know how they vote?" I said. "Because that's what you're doing."

His reply surprised me, even for him. "We'll decide what they need to see and what they don't," he said with a smile. No one else said a word. Then I watched as colleague after colleague spoke uncomfortably in support of the speaker.

Before my dustup with the speaker at the caucus meeting, I had been planning on running for chairman of the Labor, Commerce and Industry (LCI) Committee. It was an important position on a powerful committee. So earlier that summer, before the caucus met, I had gone to see the house speaker about running for the post. He had told me he liked the idea of my running, but he had also given me a big warning: He wasn't going to have a committee chairman who stepped out of line. I knew he was talking about the on-the-record-voting bill.

"I can't have a chairman that's going to question me about things," he said.

Needless to say, after the caucus meeting I knew my chances of becoming chairman of the LCI Committee were nil. I had most definitely stepped out of line as far as the speaker was concerned. The committees elected their own leadership, but the speaker still controlled committee assignments, and all the members knew it. The idea that I could get a majority on the committee to support me for chairman now was laughable. But as anyone who knows me will tell you, throwing up roadblocks in front of me only makes me work harder. Even though the chairmanship was no longer possible, the fight to get votes on the record in South Carolina was not something I was ready to give up.

I knew that if the people of South Carolina understood how pervasive anonymous voting was in the legislature, they would be with me. And later that summer, I finally got the proof I needed. A research group called the South Carolina Policy Council came out with a study that showed just how shockingly bad the lack of transparency was in South Carolina. That study showed that of all the votes taken in the house in 2008, just 8 percent were on the record. In the senate, an astounding 1 percent of all votes were recorded for the taxpayers to see.

We knew we needed to take this study and use it to let the people of South Carolina know they were being had by their elected officials. So Nathan and I, along with Governor Sanford and Ashley Landess of the Policy Council, got a little four-seater plane and did a fly-around to spread the word. In Charleston, Myrtle Beach, Greenville, and Columbia we told the people, "Did you know that only one percent of the votes in the senate were on the record this year? Did you know that our legislature is making a mockery of *your* vote by not recording *their* votes?" The people didn't know, and they were horrified. We urged them to call their senators and representatives to demand that they put their names on the bill we were introducing.

In the legislature, the leadership takes care of those who take care of them. Every committee move and assignment is fought over in many ways. If you play ball, you move up. If you don't play ball, you're powerless. After I began the on-the-record-voting push—just as he had promised—the speaker chose to use me as an example of what they do to those who step out of line.

Before the legislature convened for the new session in 2009, we first had to take care of the business of committee assignments. In the 2008 election I had been reelected by the largest margin of any legislator in the state. I got 83 percent of the vote. So even though I knew the chairmanship of the Labor, Commerce and Industry Committee wasn't going to happen, I felt pretty secure that I would retain that coveted committee assignment.

The night before we were scheduled to vote on the chairmanship in early December, I called the legislator I was running against to tell him I had decided to take myself out of the running. He took the news graciously and then he did something that surprised me: He asked me to nominate him for the chairmanship in the committee the next day. I was a little taken aback, but I said yes, of course I would. I didn't know it at the time but was later told that as he spoke to me, he was sitting next to the speaker at dinner. I was clueless, but they had a plan.

The next day the house convened and went right to the committee assignments. Although the speaker has the power to make most of the committee assignments, one committee is different, and it happens to be the Ethics Committee, which Nathan sat on. Members of the Ethics Committee are chosen by a vote of the whole house. Usually this is a pro forma vote, and if you're on the Ethics Committee, you traditionally stay on it. But that morning I watched in horror as the entire house voted to remove Nathan from the Ethics Committee. I was devastated. The leadership had put out the word that Nathan was to be punished. I knew it was because of his support of on-the-record voting—because of his support of me. I remember looking at him sitting at the desk next to me as the vote was announced. All I could say was "I'm sorry. I'm sorry."

The next order of business was the committee assignments doled out by the speaker. As the pages passed around envelopes and we all sat obediently at our desks, I felt a sense of foreboding. I looked over at Nathan as he looked at the list. He had been hoping to be promoted to the Labor, Commerce and Industry Committee with me, but he had a crestfallen look on his face as he looked at the list. Instead of being promoted, he had been demoted. The speaker had moved him from the Education Committee to the least powerful, least prestigious post of them all, the Medical, Military, Public and Municipal Affairs Committee. It was the one committee in the Republican-led house that was controlled by Democrats. Nathan would be virtually invisible there. When I looked for my name, I saw that I had kept my seat on the LCI Committee. I was confused. Why would the speaker punish Nathan and not punish me? It didn't make sense.

After we received our assignments, we were to go straight to our committee meetings. Still confused over what had happened, I reported to the LCI Committee. When I arrived, I noticed the leadership's two main staffers were there, pacing back and forth outside the committee room. This was odd, but I chalked it up to their wanting to make sure that everything went as planned and that I nominated my opponent to be chairman. What I couldn't so easily explain was the grins they had on their faces. You could tell they knew something exciting was about to happen.

After we sat down at the committee table, the motion to elect a new chairman was made. Dutifully, I rose to nominate my former competition. At that point a colleague leaned over to me and whispered, "You're a class act." That was nice to hear, but I couldn't help but think that class acts finish last. I knew I had lost the chance to be chairman because I broke the rules. I didn't kiss the ring. I didn't make the promises that needed to be made or cut the deals that needed to be cut. The representative accepted the nomination and was elected chairman. And as we adjourned, I saw the leadership's men out in the hallway, looking into the committee room and smiling. Something was definitely wrong.

I went back to my office more sad about what had happened to Nathan than about what had happened to me. After all, I was still on the committee I was most passionate about. I am a policy wonk by nature, and there is nothing I love more than to create policy that impacts the business environment of our state. Jobs are key. The goal of every state government should be to reduce taxes and regulations to make it easier for businesses to thrive, because when business thrives, jobs are created. The LCI Committee was a place where I could do that. I had already been able to help win policy battles in the committee, like workers' comp reform and coastal insurance reform. I knew I wouldn't be chairman, but at least I would still be in the mix.

When I got to the suite I shared with Nathan, I began to talk with Eileen Fogle, our dear friend, confidante, and shared assistant, about what had happened. She had seen it all and was devastated too. She had been there with us since Nathan and I were freshmen and had watched as we fought, were ridiculed, and now were being beaten down for a commonsense reform.

Then the ax fell. The chief of staff to the leadership came into my office and handed me an envelope. "The speaker has a very special letter for you," he said. I knew right then I had been set up. It all suddenly made sense. Nathan being demoted and not me. Being asked to nominate my opponent. The leering, grinning boys in the hallway outside the committee room. And now the leadership's chief of staff standing in front of me with an envelope and a barely concealed smile on his face.

A few minutes later, Nathan came into the office. I turned to him and handed him the letter that was inside the envelope:

"Effective immediately, you have been removed from the Labor, Commerce and Industry Committee."

I found out later that the leadership had removed me as majority whip as well. I was humiliated, and that was the point. When I went against the leadership, I expected to be made an example of. But this was more than just teaching a lesson. This was intended to be cruel, to burn. The speaker had the power to put members on committees and to take them off. Still, voters understand that the flip side of holding a politician's feet to the fire when he does something wrong is getting his back when he's doing what he thinks is right—even if it goes against the political grain. They understand that when petty politics gets in the middle of this process, the people's work doesn't get done. They get it.

And to make sure the people got it, I called up the Associated Press and told the whole story. Normally, these kinds of political games would be conducted off the front pages. The victims usually don't want to suffer further recrimination, so they tend to keep their mouths shut. But I knew the only way anything was going to change was if voters knew how the people they had elected to lead them were spending their time and their energy.

"I went against the speaker on something he was publicly against: votes on the record," I told AP reporter Jim Davenport. "And I was not just demoted, but he attempted to embarrass me and humiliate me in the process. What he proved in these last two days is that he is a speaker who is more concerned about his personal image than he is about policy in this state."

At the *State*, a columnist wrote simply, "Well, I guess he showed them who the big ol' hairy speaker is."

For the most part, my colleagues were kind, the Republicans and especially the Democrats. They thought what had been done showed the kind of arrogance that kills energy and destroys morale in a legislative body. I found friends I hadn't known I had, but I also discovered later that some so-called friends had taken great joy in what had happened.

What was the lesson? The night of my removal from the LCI Committee, I was at home and still pretty upset. Michael asked me if it was all worth it. "If I can't get something as simple as legislators voting on the record, I don't need to be here," I told him. "This will have been worth it when that happens." That was my way of saying that the lesson I had learned from the whole episode is that if you fight for something, you have to be prepared to lose everything in the process, but you also have to be determined to win in the end. That's how you make sure the fight is always worth it: by winning.

When the new legislative session began in January 2009, Nathan and I were blackballed. Nobody even wanted to be seen talking to us. But I was determined to continue my push for on-the-record voting anyway. The speaker was trying to make excuses for why Nathan and I had been removed from our committees, but everyone knew what the real story was. Still, people were scared. The club was the club and the rules were the rules.

Then, a couple of weeks after the 2009 session began, our movement received a needed boost. In his State of the State address, speaking before the members of the general assembly and the leadership that had fought so hard against it, Governor Sanford thanked those who had supported the fight to get votes on the record. He singled out Nathan and me and called us brave for "standing behind an issue that [we] believed in." Then he went off script and spoke a little truth to power.

"We all need to remember that the rarest of all political commodities is courage—that willingness to take a stand . . . based on something you believe in, regardless of the consequences that will come your way," he said, looking up from his speech to the members of the legislature. "As we all know, there was a price that they paid for the stand that they took, and yet change has begun as the result of the stand they took."

Governor Sanford was right. Change had begun. The people were starting to demand it. Whether it was the fight for votes on the record or the fight for more accountability in government spending, my ace in the hole was always the people. When the old guard resisted change, I went to the people to make their voices heard. It turned out that all along, those people were the Tea Party. We hadn't formally found each other yet—they didn't even call themselves the Tea Party at the time—but they were the citizens who called the radio talk shows, wrote letters to the editor, and blasted e-mails to their friends and family to bring about change in Columbia. Over time they would become my greatest friends and biggest supporters.

When I introduced my bill to get votes on the record in Columbia, it was immediately and instinctively embraced by the Tea Party. As they got the word out, Democrats began to call me and ask to have their names put on the bill. Then Republicans did as well. The bill took on a life of its own. People across the state were calling their legislators to see if they supported the bill. I had legislators coming up to me in a panic saying, "Make sure my name is on the bill!"

As I fought alongside the Tea Party to get votes on the record, I also fought with them against President Obama's stimulus bill, which had passed at the end of January as Washington's desperate attempt to boost the stagnant economy. The money promised to the states in the bill came with strings attached—long, strong strings. In the area of unemployment insurance, for example, the stimulus mandated that states change their programs to broaden eligibility—and create new costs—as a condition of receiving the money. But what would happen when the money ran out? I supported Governor Sanford in his fight for South Carolina to reject the stimulus funds because I believed the bill took our state—and our country—in exactly the wrong direction. It mandated more spending instead of less and encouraged us to avoid the difficult but necessary tasks of prioritizing the way we used taxpayers' money and reining in government.

The fight to get votes on the record was a natural part of the backlash stirred by the excesses of the stimulus bill and the antidemocratic way the Obama health-care law had been forced through that spring. Both Washington and Columbia were operating without any accountability, as if the taxpayers had no say in how their money was spent. Requiring votes on the record was about reversing that by putting power back in the hands of the people. But despite how much popular support the bill aroused, it took a long time to change the law in South Carolina. Almost a year after I introduced the bill, it was finally passed in the statehouse, and even then the old guard couldn't resist playing games with it. I was running for governor by then, and the leadership waited until they knew I had left the chamber for an event in Greenville before they brought the bill up and quickly passed it before I could get back. Evidently they wanted to make it look like I was neglecting my duties in the legislature by missing the vote. They got what they wanted. The next day there were stories in the newspapers saying I wasn't even there for the passage of my own bill.

I made getting votes on the record a central part of my campaign for governor. I talked about it in every speech and at every campaign event. More than any other single issue, this fight epitomized what had motivated me to run for governor. I believe people should have the right to know what their elected officials are doing, because elected officials work for the people, not the other way around.

The establishment had thrown up a lot of roadblocks, but in the end the people of South Carolina won the day. On April 12, 2011, after I'd become governor, I signed the bill into law. That day, as I waited for the signing ceremony to begin, I texted Nathan that this day had been a long time coming. Who knew the same legislators who had been blackballed, demoted, and humiliated would be sharing this victory with the people of South Carolina? Finally my chief of staff, Tim Pearson, came into my office and said, "Ready to make history today?"

Nathan and I and other legislators who had helped push the bill forward walked out to the statehouse lobby with Pat Benatar's "Hit Me with Your Best Shot" pumping through the sound system. The room was full of constituents who had fought side by side with us. They had carried our message. They had sent the e-mails, called in to radio shows, and yelled their support at Tea Party rallies. They had fought for three years. There was never any question of their not being there at the end for the signing. This had been as much their fight as ours.

There were loud cheers and applause. This wasn't just another bill signing. It was a celebration. It marked the end of an era of unaccountable spending and backroom deal making and the beginning of a new era of government of the people, by the people, and for the people. It was history in the making.

I stood there and spoke from the podium. In the audience were those who had supported us all along the way, as well as members of the house leadership who had fought us every step of the way. Everyone wanted in on the celebration, and we were happy to have them.

This was a victory for South Carolina. We weren't going to play political games with it. We'd had enough of political games.

"This is about accountability in South Carolina," I told the fired-up crowd. "This would not have happened without the will of the people. This is what happens when people care about their government. This is your day."

It was true. The day didn't belong to me. It belonged to the people. I looked out and saw my parents, and I thought of what they had always taught me: If you fight for the right things, God will take care of the rest. It had taken a while, but in the end my parents were right. The people had fought. Their cause was just. And now God was smiling down on South Carolina.

I signed the bill. Then I took the pen and handed it to Nathan. "No one sacrificed and lost more than you did in this fight," I said. He will hate my saying this, but I saw tears in his eyes at that press conference. But it's okay, because I had them too.

Chapter Five

Are They Ready?

The fight to get legislative votes on the record in South Carolina was both inspiring and demoralizing. It was inspiring because we were winning—the people of South Carolina were winning—on an issue that is at the heart of representative democracy. But it was also depressing because of how hard it was to move forward on an issue that is at the heart of representative democracy. Just introducing the bill had cost me every leadership position I had.

By 2009 I had some hard thinking to do about my future as a state representative. I loved my work and I loved representing the people of the 87th District. But the on-the-record-voting campaign had cost me. As long as the leadership was against me, I had lost any ability to move any other legislation through the house. And as for moving up the food chain in terms of committee assignments or leadership posts, well . . . you don't need to hit me over the head with a brick *twice* to send me the message.

My dilemma was no secret to folks in Columbia. People kept asking me to run for state treasurer. They profiled me as an accountant and thought it would be a good fit and an "easy win" for me. The problem was that I wasn't interested. I know numbers, but I love policy. I love finding ways to make people's lives better. I needed to continue to challenge myself in a way that would allow me to get results.

At the start of the legislative session, I had a meeting with Governor Sanford to discuss a couple of issues. It was pretty routine at first. We went through the items on the agenda, and then he asked me how things were going. I told him everything was fine. I updated him on the progress we were making on the roll-call-vote front. And I mentioned that I was being encouraged to run for treasurer. "But I don't think I'll do it," I said. "I'm good when I'm passionate about something. And I know my heart wouldn't be in being treasurer."

Governor Sanford and I shared a commitment to limited government and reform, but he was a hard person to get to know. He called me "Nikki" and I called him "Governor." I respected him for his policies, but I was never quite sure what he was going to do next. In our conversation that day, he surprised me again.

He agreed I shouldn't run for treasurer. "I think you should run for governor," he said.

I immediately started cracking up. "I can't run for governor. I've only been in office five years." He said that didn't matter. And then he said the words that I will never forget.

"You fight for what you believe in. You don't back down from a fight," said Governor Sanford. "You're tough and you're a lot nicer than I am."

It was then that I realized he was serious. He was term limited and couldn't run again. He was telling me he wanted me to take the reins of the reform movement.

"Governor," I said, "do you think South Carolina is ready for a female governor?"

"No, but they're ready for you."

I will never forget that moment. How cool.

Governor Sanford's encouragement meant a lot to me. He was the closest thing South Carolina politics had to a rock star in the spring of 2009. Congress had passed President Obama's bloated stimulus bill a few months earlier, and Governor Sanford had waged a fierce (and ultimately unsuccessful) battle against the spending, even against its funding for South Carolina. His principled, fiscally conservative stand didn't sit too well with the national media or the South Carolina establishment, but it made him a hero to many South Carolinians and others across the country. He was also, at the time, the chairman of the powerful Republican Governors Association (RGA). His connections and fund-raising ability would be a godsend to an unknown, underdog candidate.

Most important to me was the fact that Governor Sanford was at the forefront of something that I came to call "the Movement." Put simply, the Movement is about making government work for the people rather than the other way around. Governor Sanford was a leading force of the Movement. Not only did he fight the stimulus, but he also fought the Washington bailouts, whether they were of the banks or the auto companies. He was Tea Party before there was a Tea Party, fighting for government to live within its means and be accountable to the people. For South Carolina, Mark Sanford was the right governor at the right time. To have him suggest that I run for governor—even tacitly offer his support—was both humbling and exciting.

What I didn't know then was that it was the governor's better half, his then wife Jenny, who had believed in me first. She was a strong force behind him in many ways and a strong early supporter of mine.

Where Governor Sanford could be mercurial and unpredictable, Jenny was focused and dependable. Only a couple months later, under the most trying of circumstances, South Carolina and much of the rest of America would learn just how wise, courageous, and graceful Jenny Sanford was. Throughout my campaign, during what was a tremendous personal travail for her, she remained a steadfast advocate and friend to me. I will always be grateful to her.

As I left that meeting with Governor Sanford, I thought about what he had said. Should I run for governor? My campaign five years earlier against Larry Koon instantly came to my mind. *This time*, I thought, *I should look before I leap, right?* But when I actually looked, what I saw wasn't much better than finding out that half the district was related to Mr. Koon. By May 2009 three well-established politicians had either thrown their hats into the ring for the Republican nomination or were about to. South Carolina's attorney general, Henry McMaster, and South Carolina congressman Gresham Barrett, were the presumed front-runners. As if these two weren't formidable enough, our lieutenant governor, André Bauer, was also seeking the Republican nomination. All three had high name recognition and extensive political and fund-raising networks. All three were seasoned pols backed by South Carolina's notoriously tough political professionals. And me? Well, I was "Nikki who?" all over again.

My ace in the hole, such as it was, was Governor Sanford. I was extremely comforted by the thought of having his support and endorsement. I had struggled all my life for anything I had ever received. The idea that this time I would have help was overwhelming to me. At the time, Governor Sanford had an 80 percent approval rating among Republicans in the state and a growing reputation nationwide. There was talk of his making a presidential run. I would have to do the work, but I knew that his star power would boost my credibility and visibility and give me a big financial leg up once I started fund-raising. *I might even learn what it's like to fight on a level playing field for a change,* I thought.

I talked to Michael. And just as he had when I decided to run for the state house, he didn't ask why, he just jumped into the decision making with me. Our first thoughts were for our two kids, Rena, then ten, and Nalin, seven. I remembered the state house campaign and dreaded putting my family through anything like that again. But I am blessed with two amazing children and a husband who supports me unconditionally. Michael is the best husband and father I know. He's a military man. He puts on the uniform of an Army National Guardsman every day because he loves our state and our country. But he loves his family more. I am successful because of the love of my family but more than anything because of Michael's patience and support. We talked through the potential minefields of a gubernatorial campaign and decided to go for it. He's my partner. For Michael as much as me, "can't" was not an option.

With the truly important decisions out of the way, I went to see B. J. Boling and Walter Whetsell, a South Carolina consultant who had helped me in the state house runoff. Everything I had done in my six years in public service I had done with the advice of these two. They were my comrades-in-arms during the house race. We had been through the war together. I knew their families. I had attended the wedding of one and the funeral of a family member of the other. I considered them my friends. So it was with great hurt that I discovered they weren't going to be with me in the run for governor. They had already been contacted by Congressman Barrett's campaign and had decided to go with him. The people I considered to be the closest to me in my political life would be the ones working against me in what would be the biggest political challenge of my life.

I had never been a great fan of political consultants, but this experience really soured me for a while on the profession. I came away from it thinking that for consultants politics is just a game. They play for whoever's paying them at the time, and then they move on. There never is any real loyalty, and I have a big problem with treating politics and public office like a game. Winning isn't the be-all and end-all for me. I want to get things done.

Still, I guess it's possible that my natural distrust of political consultants could have something to do with my being stubborn. I don't like anybody trying to tell me what to say or how to think. I believe in trusting my gut. For good or for ill, my intuition usually dictates what I do. Too often political consultants think selling candidates is like selling soap—follow the formula and read the three-by-five cards and you will win. I never liked the idea of being packaged and sold.

I realized that contemplating a run for governor without some professional help was out of the question. A friend recommended that I talk to a young, newly hired staffer for Governor Sanford named Tim Pearson. I liked Tim immediately. He was from Connecticut. He'd only been working for Sanford for a few months, so he was outside the South Carolina political bubble. I liked that. I wanted someone who could see Columbia through fresh eyes, someone who wasn't so invested in the establishment.

Tim and I met at Starbucks and talked for about an hour. He was young but obviously very bright. Truth be told, Tim would come to reveal to me talents that I didn't grasp initially. I hired him to be my communications director, but he ended up being my campaign manager, finance director, communications director, and office manager. More than that—much more than that—he challenged my stubborn streak about political consultants. Tim didn't try to make me change my principles or be something I'm not. It was never about him. It was always about the team and the Movement. Throughout the campaign, he gave his all, every day, seven days a week, twenty-four hours a day. Skeptics said the fact that he wasn't from South Carolina was a liability—he didn't know the game, they said. But Tim is like me: When he's presented with a challenge, he forces himself to rise to it. His "game" was messaging and policy, not tearing down opponents and engaging in political gossip. I think he showed everyone that maybe the inside game is what's wrong with the process.

Tim had committed to staying on with Governor Sanford through the end of the legislative session in June, and I respected that. I still needed help with polling and advertising, though, and that is how I came upon a remarkable political thinker named Jon Lerner.

Jon had worked closely with Governor Sanford in his campaigns, and he was still working with Sanford when I first spoke to him. Initially, I worried that I wouldn't be able to get along with him. We are in many ways complete opposites. Where I follow my gut, Jon relies on facts and the statistics he finds in his polling. I used to call him a lemon because he never got excited about anything. I would go on and on about the things I thought were great—this or that award, my associations with different groups, or my conservative record. He thought that was great too, he would say, but where were my numbers? I would get excited about the small stuff. "Jon, I came in third in the straw poll!" "Um . . . okay," he would say. "I'm glad you think they matter." Jon is principled and he understands what it takes to put principles into action. As I would learn later, he is Jewish and observes the Sabbath. Even in the heat of a campaign, he never works from sundown Friday to sundown Saturday. His faith, I think, gives him a great perspective on what really matters and what doesn't. He could care less about the political bubble. He uses facts and statistics to promote the people and the principles he believes in.

So it was no accident that I first met Jon at the end of April during a visit to the governor's mansion to go over a poll he had conducted for Governor Sanford.

Michael and I drove over that night, and Governor Sanford, Jenny, and Jon were there. I was excited to take a look at what the poll had to say about the race and my potential candidacy. For the first (but not for the last!) time, Jon brought me back down to earth. The poll showed that I would start the race with just 3 percent of the voters' support. That's not a typo: 3 percent. While that news was rather deflating, I was sort of encouraged when Jon explained that he thought there was a pathway to victory for me despite the long odds. If I was going to run, I had a lot of work to do. I knew then that Jon was the steadying, analytical force I needed to keep my eyes on the prize.

I remember that evening for another reason as well. After having encouraged my run and been generous with his time and his advice, Governor Sanford was once again strangely distant. While Jenny, Jon, Michael, and I pored over the data inside the mansion, he went outside and exercised. Jenny, in his absence, was insightful and engaged. Again and again I asked the governor for different ways he could help my campaign, and again and again he was noncommittal. I remember leaving the mansion that night with a creeping sense of panic. I knew that it was my race to win or lose, but I was relying on Governor Sanford's support. "I'm not going to do this," I told Michael during the car ride home. "I don't mind working hard, but if he's not going to help, what chance do I have?"

The next day, after I'd slept on it, I talked to Jon. I was deeply disappointed in the meeting with the governor, I told him, and I had real reservations about running when he was being so noncommittal. I thought we were both members in good standing of the Movement, I said. Why wasn't he with me? Jon promised to go talk to the governor. A couple days later, Governor Sanford called and said he was going to write down a list of things he would do for me—"just so you can't say I didn't do the things I promised," he said. It was classic Sanford. Supportive but strangely emotionally distant. I got the letter a few days later.

*   *   *

After all the pondering and preparation, on May 14 I just did it. Tim still worked for Governor Sanford, so he wasn't there. Jon was in Maryland. Thank goodness Michael was there. I was the most nervous I'd been in a long time. What would they think? Would they think I was qualified? Were they ready for a girl in the governor's office? How would the political establishment react? I was announcing my campaign for governor of South Carolina.

A friend with a construction company let me borrow his conference room. There had been speculation that I would announce a run, but no one was quite sure. We had a legislative session that day, and I remember everyone kept coming to Nathan to get the skinny on what was going on. He sat right next to me on the floor of the house, of course. We always laughed about how people stopped by his desk to ask him questions or make comments about me when I was sitting right there next to him.

Back in the conference room, it was just me, Michael, my scheduler, and some of the print media from around the state. "For more than five years I've sat in the statehouse and watched—sometimes in disbelief—as our state government has spent with abandon and in the process wasted taxpayer dollar after taxpayer dollar," I told the assembled reporters. "I know what good government can look like. I'm running for governor so the people of the state will know what it feels like."

And with that, I was in.

After the announcement there was a frenzy of media calls. I've always gotten attention at first when I take on new challenges because I'm Indian American and because I'm female. But I've always known that kind of attention is short-lived—and beside the point. I wasn't there because my parents came from India or because I was female. I had real things I wanted to accomplish for South Carolina. But I had to overcome the "Nikki who?" hurdle first. And this fact, by the way, was not lost on the press.

I was "a relative unknown" who "starts at a fundraising disadvantage," reported a local newspaper.

CNN reported that I would become South Carolina's first female governor—"if she can survive a crowded Republican primary already loaded with South Carolina GOP heavyweights who are backed by some of the state's best political strategists."

Roll Call, the Capitol Hill newspaper, got right to the point: "Haley will have a tough time trumping the name ID of statewide officeholders like McMaster and Bauer."

There was good news too, though. While stopping short of endorsing me, Governor Sanford put out a statement calling me "one of our state's leading voices for fiscal responsibility and government reform." I was very appreciative of his words of encouragement.

That day calls poured in from South Carolinians who wanted to help. I had set up a Web site where people could sign up to volunteer, get yard signs, or make donations. Hundreds of people were logging on. I began to allow myself to hope that we had tapped into something real in the grass roots of South Carolina.

Then I got a call. Our Web site had been taken down. People trying to log on to sign up for the campaign weren't getting in. The names of hundreds of supporters were being lost. Instantly I knew the reason. The person who had built my Web site was also the Web site and social-media consultant of my opponent in the primary, Congressman Gresham Barrett. I had foolishly paid him to create my Web site and social-media outlets. What should have been a great day of collecting names was ruined by political dirty tricks.

It was a taste of what was to come, but there was no turning back. I was in. Just as before, the only option now was to win.

Chapter Six
The Sanford Implosion

Governor Sanford was giddy.

He's not what you would call a giddy guy, but that morning he was positively bursting with energy and good humor. It was June 17, and my campaign for governor was in full swing. Tim was now on staff full time, and he and I had come to the governor's mansion to take some pictures with Governor Sanford. Overall, things were going as well as could be expected. Even though we were still far behind our competition in name recognition, we were raising money at a respectable clip. Jon was on board and we were starting to get our message out. These photos with the governor, I thought, would help us with fund-raising. They were the kind of boost we needed to help fire up our underdog campaign.

But what was with the governor? As we posed for shots inside the mansion and outside under the elm trees, this normally aloof, distant man was playful and goofy. He was vamping for the camera and making jokes. Tim and I exchanged looks. "What was that?" I asked him as we got in the car to leave that day. Neither of us had seen the governor in such a strange mood before. We had no way of knowing then the reason for his good humor. He was on the verge of taking a trip that would have lasting implications for his family and career. Thanks to what was to happen in the coming days, we would never see the pictures we took that morning. They were all but worthless.

I was scheduled to go to Washington, D.C., in a few days to engage in a ritual of American politics: meeting with the influential donors, reporters, and political analysts. We had two days of meetings scheduled. My job was to convince a slew of people who had never heard of me that I was a serious contender for governor.

The trip was a blur of conference rooms, men and women in suits, and pitching my case. For the most part, everyone seemed interested in what I could bring to the governorship. There were exceptions, however. One of the most memorable was my meeting with a political analyst named Stuart Rothenberg. I went into the meeting excited to tell him about my race and how I was going to change South Carolina. His response shocked me. Skepticism I could take—skepticism was what I *expected*. But he was combative and rude. "Do people see you as (a) black, (b) white, or (c) other?" he asked. That was it. I was completely offended and I told him so. The conversation only went downhill from there. I got a lecture afterward from Tim and Jon about how I couldn't talk back to these kinds of people. My response was simple. If they won't ask stupid questions, I won't talk back to them.

While we were in Washington, the news back home became increasingly focused on the governor. Where was Mark Sanford? He had been missing for four days, since the day after our photo shoot at the mansion. By our second day in D.C., the story had gone national and was blanketing the cable news. Sanford's staff was reporting that he was taking some time to recharge by hiking the Appalachian Trail. This sounded believable to me. Governor Sanford was quirky like that. He loved the outdoors, and he was something of an introvert; it didn't surprise me that he would go off alone. He also had a long history of ditching his security detail. Besides, he had just been through a tough battle on the Obama stimulus bill. Hiking the Appalachian Trail seemed like something our governor would do. It was odd, though, I thought, that they couldn't reach him.

My last day in Washington was filled with the by-now-familiar meetings. In between appointments, I caught a news report on Governor Sanford on the television in the waiting room. The story was still focused on where the governor could be. But that day there was a new, more ominous development. After initially saying she was sure he was just taking some time away from the kids to write, Jenny Sanford changed her tone and her message. "I am being a mom today," she told CNN. "I have not heard from my husband. I am taking care of my children." Clearly, something was not right. I called Jon.

"Something's wrong, Jon, I can feel it," I said. "Jenny would never have responded that way if there weren't something wrong." Jon didn't answer me, but he didn't have to. I could hear from the sound of his voice that he agreed.

I finished my last meeting and happened to see Mississippi governor Haley Barbour on the ride down in the elevator. "Where's your governor?" he asked. "On the Appalachian Trail," I answered sheepishly. But I had a pit in my stomach. I knew what I was saying was probably not true.

I got home that night and spoke to Jon. "It's not good," he said. "The news will be bad tomorrow. Just hunker down until we can figure it all out." I woke up the next morning and was heading into my job at the Lexington Medical Center Foundation, where I now worked when the house wasn't in session, when I got a call from Tim. "The governor was in Argentina," he said. "We just got a call from a news station asking if you were with him." I felt sick to my stomach.

I turned around on the steps of the hospital and went immediately back to the office. When I got there, Tim intercepted me in the parking lot. "I want you to know what's going on," he said. The media were reporting that they had found Governor Sanford's car at the airport. "They have sources watching the airport, and your car was spotted parked next to the governor's," Tim continued. "We told the station they can't run the story. We told them you were in D.C. and not anywhere near the governor."

Even after the days of speculation, I couldn't believe what I was hearing. Why was the governor in Argentina? I thought of his staff and friends, whom he'd allowed to tell what he knew were lies about his whereabouts. I thought of Jenny and her boys, and the betrayal her comments increasingly reflected. And I thought with horror about how I was now being dragged into this scandal. For the first time I came face-to-face with what it meant to be a woman in the race. The rumor about Governor Sanford and me lacked any factual foundation whatsoever. I had been in meetings for days in D.C. with dozens of people—including holding on-the-record, already published interviews with reporters. But the fact that the media were even asking said it all. They wouldn't be putting a male candidate in the humiliating position of having to explain why his car was parked by chance next to the governor's at the airport. I couldn't believe this was happening in 2009 in America.

Tim managed to convince the now-ravenous media that I hadn't been in Argentina with the governor, but in the hours and days that followed the scandal only got worse. That morning a local reporter, acting on an anonymous tip, met Governor Sanford as he stepped off a flight from Buenos Aires. Later that day, back in Columbia, the governor held an emotional press conference. He confessed to being unfaithful to his wife and traveling to Argentina to meet his mistress. He had met her eight years earlier, he said, but their relationship had become romantic only the previous year. Jenny, he said, had discovered the affair five months earlier, in January. Despite her repeated warnings not to see the woman again, he had once again ditched his security detail and drove himself to the airport, parking next to where I would park for my trip to D.C. For six days he had lied to his family and lied to South Carolinians. Now, alone at the podium outside his office in the statehouse, he was asking for forgiveness.

The news electrified the media and Governor Sanford's political opponents. You could watch, in real time, as a man who had had an 80 percent approval rating just days earlier exploded before your eyes.

Later that day, Jenny announced that she had asked the governor to move out of their home in Sullivan's Island two weeks earlier. Even in her very public pain, she was a perfect example of grace and strength. Her first thoughts were always for her boys. She said she still loved her husband and, because of her four boys, had worked for months to save her marriage. And despite all the betrayal she had suffered, she remained committed to her marriage. I remember praying for her and her boys, for the entire Sanford family, to have strength during this time of very public betrayal.

In the days that followed, the governor gave a series of ill-advised interviews in which he called the woman in Argentina his "soul mate," spoke of trying to "fall back in love" with his wife, and confessed that there were other women he had "crossed lines" with. Tim and I called Jon and begged him to ask the governor to just stop talking. And for the first time, I felt anger toward the man I had seen as a leader in our fight for conservative reform. Why hadn't he told me about all this when he encouraged me to run for governor just months earlier? Why had he let me jump into the race knowing that this might happen? I was angry, but mostly I felt sorry for him and Jenny. The *State* gleefully published the salacious e-mails sent between the governor and the Argentine woman. To this day I have refused to read those e-mails. Having such a personal crisis play out nationally and to have their faces and their names blared all over the airwaves in such a negative way was brutal for Governor Sanford and especially Jenny. I would come to know later just how brutal it was. I wouldn't wish it on anyone.

Next to the wreckage of the Sanford family, the political fallout of the scandal was less important but no less severe. Governor Sanford was forced to immediately resign his position as head of the Republican Governors Association. Any presidential aspirations he had, needless to say, were gone. And even though he insisted he had no plans to step down as governor of South Carolina, his career in state politics seemed to be effectively over.

As for my campaign, we had lost a potential base of support, it was true. But much more devastating than that was the fact that we had lost a philosophical stalwart. Whatever you thought of Mark Sanford personally—and he had done a lot to discredit himself as a husband— he had started a discussion about the role of government that resonated not just in our state but across the country. He had felt the wrath of his own party establishment, standing virtually alone against the corruption of the stimulus and the bailouts. Years before the Tea Party took the call from coast to coast, he had awoken South Carolina to the dangers of out-of-control spending and out-of-touch government. It was this legacy of reform that I had hoped to continue in the governor's office. But now it looked like that legacy would be a casualty of the implosion that had rocked Governor Sanford's professional and personal lives. And in the wake of that implosion, it looked like my campaign would be a casualty too.

The aftermath of the Sanford implosion, as we came to call it, was a low point for my campaign. I had gone from being an underdog with potential to being the expected endorsee of a political joke. My critics had long called me "Mark Sanford in a skirt," but now it held a special sting—and a special stigma. People looked at me with pity. They no longer treated me like a real candidate.

Worst of all, no one returned my calls. The early part of any political campaign is the money chase. This is the period when you have to raise the funds that will pay for the media and other things you will need when the real battle starts later, closer to the election, when most voters start paying attention. Before Sanford imploded, my fundraising had been respectable. In the six weeks since I had become a candidate, my team and I had raised more than $200,000. I had always been a relentless fund-raiser. In my state house race, I had walked into rooms full of uncommitted voters and routinely left with thousand-dollar checks. But in the aftermath of the Sanford scandal, I couldn't raise a dime. People were disgusted with the governor and scared of me. They associated me with him, and they just wanted to put the whole mess behind them.

When people did call, the news was invariably bad. One of the Republican kingmakers I had met with on my trip to D.C., who had told me he might be able to help out my campaign, called to tell me he wouldn't be helping after all. With Sanford self-immolating, he said, he didn't think I could win. My response was impulsive but heart-felt. If I was worth supporting before, I said, why wasn't I worth supporting now? I told him our country would never be right until we supported people we thought *should* win rather than people we thought *could* win.

It was a bad time. Jon came to me about a month after the implosion and told me I had a decision to make. He said I was a single-digit candidate, and my prospects in this race, while not impossible, were bleak. I could stay in the race to make contacts for the next race I might run, or I could shift over to the treasurer's race. "You can get your name recognition up and your finance list built for when you want to run for something else," he said. I knew what he was saying, and I categorically rejected it. I knew the fight was going to be hard, but running just to run—without trying to win—did not interest me at all.

"Jon, I don't want to do this again. I don't want to run for something else," I told him. "I am running for governor because I don't think any of the other candidates can take this state where I can. If I don't win this, I'm getting out of public office."

Jon was just being his completely forthright, brutally honest self. He wanted me to know that the road to victory would be steep—not insurmountable—but completely uphill. "We can do this, Jon," I reassured him. "I don't know how yet, but we will win." All he said was "Okay," in his usual, unemotional way.

Looking back, I can't fault Jon for his pessimism. Morale at the campaign really took a hit after the Sanford implosion. But the hardest hit of all, I think, was Jon. Governor Sanford had been his client since 2001, and Jon considered him and Jenny friends. For a few months after the scandal broke, Jon kind of checked out on me. He still called in every other day like clockwork, but the disappointment rang in his voice. I could feel him slipping away for a while. Truth be told, he could have left me then and he probably should have. He had other clients to worry about and other—winnable—races to devote his time to. But he didn't leave, and he earned my total respect for that.

The same was true of Tim. He went through a depressed phase after the Sanford scandal. For the longest time I could tell he was holding it back, but one day he finally just said what he was feeling. "I just don't know how to get us through this. I don't know how we can win." I think we were all feeling that way. What I will forever appreciate is that Tim didn't give up. He still gave the campaign his all—despite the fact that he got engaged to and married a wonderful girl in the middle of it. He too could have taken his considerable talents to other, more viable candidates in less foreign and unrelenting political settings. But he didn't, and I will never forget that.

Jon and Tim taught me something after the Sanford implosion: Not all political consultants are the same, and Jon and Tim were certainly different from any I had ever known. There is a purpose to what they do. They believe in conservative candidates. And I would like to think that I taught them a thing or two as well. I hope I taught them that passion may be impossible to find in a poll, but it is a great asset. And I hope I taught them that nothing is ever truly impossible.

As the days and weeks passed after his scandal was revealed, Governor Sanford refused to step down. Even as members of the legislature announced they would pursue criminal and legislative investigations—and even go as far as the Justice Department in Washington, D.C.—Governor Sanford insisted he would serve out the remaining eighteen months of his term. By the first week in July, a majority of the senate had called on him to resign, but still he hung on. For my part, I tried to shift the focus back to the reform agenda and away from the tabloid details of the scandal.

Almost alone among political figures in the state, I did not push him to resign or be impeached. "The people of South Carolina have heard enough about the governor's personal life," I said at that time. "We do not need to hear any more of that. What we do need to hear from the governor is an explanation as to how he can lead our state going forward. He has a responsibility to outline what he wants to accomplish over the next eighteen months and how he intends to accomplish it."

"I remain willing to listen to that case," I said, "but if he cannot make it convincingly, then he must move on."

You could say that Governor Sanford was lucky in his timing. The legislature had just recessed when the scandal broke. When the issue of impeachment was raised, some of the legislators maintained that the rules didn't allow an impeachment vote until the legislature reconvened in January 2010. Still, the impeachment bandwagon really gained steam after it was revealed that Governor Sanford had also seen his mistress on a state-funded trade mission to Argentina in 2008. Even though the governor subsequently reimbursed the state more than three thousand dollars for these trips, the state Ethics Commission launched an investigation, as did the state attorney general's office.

As the calls for his impeachment grew louder and the governor continued to hang on to his office, I was bombarded with questions about my onetime political ally. I refused to support his impeachment even though I was basically alone among my colleagues in the house in doing so. I took this stance not because politically I thought I should (the politics of defending him were awful for me) but because I didn't think what he had done was an impeachable offense. As reprehensible as his actions were, I said, they didn't rise to the level of fraud or criminal activity that would warrant impeachment. I took a lot of heat for my stand. And I knew that the longer the scandal dragged on, the worse it would be for me. I was Mark Sanford in a dress, after all. As long as he clung to power in Columbia, no one would want a possible repeat of his administration with me. But the law was the law, and I didn't believe Governor Sanford, for all his betrayal and all his lies, had violated it. In the end, a majority of the members of a house impeachment panel agreed with me.

At the same time I was being criticized for refusing to back impeachment, I was also getting hit for taking Governor Sanford's picture off of my Web site. We had scrolling pictures on our Web site, one of which was of Governor Sanford with his quote from the day I announced, calling me one of the state's leading voices for fiscal responsibility and reform. We took the picture and the quote down the day he returned from Argentina.

As soon as we removed the picture, the media erupted with reports that I had "scrubbed all evidence" of Governor Sanford from my Web site. I never understood that charge. I had been betrayed just as much as most South Carolinians, aside from Jenny and the governor's family. Didn't I have a right to be disappointed too? I didn't have any illusions about my association with the governor. In fact, I never stopped fighting for the openness and accountability in government that he championed. Never once. But I thought I had the right, when the pain of his betrayal was still raw, to express my disappointment in him and my outrage at the damage he had done to a movement we both cherished.

So I defended him from impeachment and took press hits for taking his picture off my Web site. And after weeks of battling on two fronts and watching everyone check out on the campaign and on me, I decided I needed to go see Governor Sanford. It took me a few days to get to see him. He was still living in the mansion, while Jenny and their boys had been at the Sullivan's Island home all summer. But in August Jenny came up to Columbia and moved their things out for good.

I was nervous going into the meeting with Sanford. I didn't know what kind of shape he would be in. I didn't know what I would say. I knew that yelling at him wouldn't help either of us, but I was angry with him and I wanted to express it. He had put the agenda we had both bled for on life support. His selfishness had hurt people. I had a speech all ready to go as I drove to the statehouse to meet him in the governor's office. But as soon as I walked into the room, all of my anger stayed at the door. I saw a man who was broken. He looked like he hadn't slept in days.

I asked him how he was. "I've had better days," he said. I found myself reverting back to what I used to do—what I'd always seemed to do—when I met with him before: trying to cheer him up. All my anger was being replaced by sorrow and nostalgia. I had been a supporter of his for years. It was hard to see the leader I had believed in so weakened and so vulnerable.

But I was there for a reason. I told him I needed his help. He began to apologize to me. I stopped him. I didn't want him to do that or need him to do that. I wanted to win my race so I could carry on what we both believed in.

"Governor, I'm sorry you're going through a hard time. I know you're trying to move on," I said. "But I'm stuck. I'm still in this race. I have no money. I have no governor to endorse me anymore. I have given up my house seat. I'm totally committed to this thing. I need you to reengage."

His eyes had a glassy look. It didn't seem like anything I was saying was penetrating. He asked me what I wanted from him. I told him I needed him to make some calls, remind people that even though he had messed up I was still in the fight; I still needed their support. He looked at me and said, "I don't know that anyone will call me back."

"Governor, I have given up everything to do this." I could feel myself getting emotional. "I need you to understand that while everyone is dealing with all of your world, I am still here. I am still running for governor. I am barely staying above water."

"I know and I'm sorry," was his reply.

I left devastated. It was painful to see him the way he was. His mistakes were his and his alone, but for five years I had worked with him to restructure South Carolina's backward government and make our politicians more accountable and our state more taxpayer friendly. Some people might have been able to walk away from that without a look back and without any regret, but I couldn't. He had once singled Nathan and me out among our colleagues and said that "the rarest of all political commodities is courage." Rarer still, I think, is loyalty. What Governor Sanford had done was reprehensible. But what he had stood for still had my loyalty. Seeing him brought so low was beyond disappointing.

Chapter Seven
Underdog

One of my favorite things to say is "Get excited!" I say this all the time, at everything from bill signings to speeches to talks with groups of schoolkids. I open Facebook posts with it. Get excited! Okay, it's cheesy. But most of the time it expresses a fundamental part of my personality. I am by nature energetic and optimistic. Normally I am excited about new challenges, about the prospect of finding ways to help people.

The weeks following the Sanford explosion were not normal times. I didn't say my trademark catchphrase too much. It was difficult to get motivated when everything looked so bleak. The little campaign staff I had was bummed out and checked out. No money people would return my calls. The press referred to me, when they referred to me at all, with a dismissive tone. I was not excited.

I found myself not wanting to go into our campaign offices in West Colombia. I had managed to convince my longtime friend and supporter, Ted McGee—"Mr. Ted" I called him—to donate a three-room space in a strip mall across the river to serve as our campaign headquarters. It was in what a real estate agent would call a "transitional" neighborhood. Homeless people regularly came in to get "Haley for Governor" T-shirts. One evening, when a member of my campaign staff got back to the office late after an event in downtown Columbia, he was approached by a "woman of the night."

The office itself looked like it had last been redecorated in the 1970s, which was probably true. The walls were covered with wood paneling. What furniture we had was scuffed up and mismatched. The bathroom was in the middle of the space, and the walls were paper thin. There was absolutely no privacy (the staff took to using the facilities at the Subway down the street). If you wanted to have a private conversation, you had to go outside. Tim and I would routinely haul the vintage kitchen chairs that served as our desk chairs out into the parking lot to sit and talk.

Even though my staff thought our office had a . . . let's just say "rustic" feel, I loved it. To me it screamed everything our campaign was. Underdog. Shoestring. Taking on the establishment. Every time I walked in I was reminded that I was in fourth place. No one expected me to win, and boy, were they going to be surprised when I did.

In the days and weeks after the Sanford scandal broke, that feisty, fighting spirit left me for a while. And then one morning I woke up. I didn't want to go into my seventies-style office, but I did. I started working and getting creative. I told the staff we were going to have fun. When you have nothing to lose, it's amazing how much fun you can have trying to win.

We turned all our campaign's shortcomings into strengths. Traditional political campaign theory told us we couldn't win—we didn't have enough in the bank to be competitive. We disagreed with that concept. For us it wasn't how much money we had but how we spent it that mattered. So when the donations dried up after the Sanford explosion, we worked out a strategy. Every dollar we could raise would go to television. We knew we were at a huge disadvantage in name recognition. No one outside Lexington County knew who I was, whereas my opponents were all well known. Our hurdle wasn't our message—there was no doubt in my mind that South Carolina was ready for a governor who would take on the good-old-boy, back-scratching political culture in Columbia. Our hurdle was getting our message out to the people and letting them know we were there. Doing that meant television, and television cost money. So we lived off the land and saved all we could for TV ads.

Michael had previously owned a barter company, and I had a background in business. Together we put what we had learned in the private sector to work for the campaign. We knew it was easier for businesses to donate products to us as opposed to money, so we survived on in-kind donations. Every aspect of our campaign, except utilities and salaries, was donated. Our dingy furniture came from home or was donated. The printers and fax machines were donated. When we were on the road, we usually stayed with relatives, friends, and supporters who were willing to put us up. Our campaign events were catered by restaurants I had convinced to donate food.

Other campaigns had fancy signs everywhere. The state was festooned with BARRETT FOR GOVERNOR yard signs. Large MCMASTER FOR GOVERNOR four-by-eight signs lined the highways. We couldn't afford yard signs, so I suggested that we sell them. My campaign staff was horrified at this concept. This was something that just wasn't done! "You can't charge people for yard signs," they said. "No one will buy them." My response was simple. One, we don't have a choice because we don't have the money for signs. Two, if a person actually pays for a sign, he or she is a lot more likely to care about keeping the sign and about promoting the candidate whose name is on the sign. And three,

I'll bet if we ask our supporters to pay for signs, they'll do it. Turns out I was right. We sold our signs for five dollars apiece; if you bought four, you got one free! They were a big hit. I think we might be the only campaign in South Carolina history to have actually turned a profit on yard signs. What was really crazy was that later on, when our campaign started to catch fire and draw national attention, we had people from all over the country willing to pay for our signs. I still scratch my head when I think of the guy in Toledo, Ohio, who had a NIKKI HALEY FOR SOUTH CAROLINA GOVERNOR sign in his yard.

Another unique aspect of our underdog campaign was staff. The other campaigns had dozens of people working for them, whereas over time I built a small but powerful campaign staff. Besides Tim and Jon and me, it consisted of three paid workers and the occasional intern we could talk into working for free. In addition to my family, they were the secret to my success. I hope one day my campaign will be a lesson to candidates everywhere. Politicos will always tell you that you will fail if you don't have a certain amount of money, signs, endorsements, or staff. But I found out that all of that can be made up for with smart decisions and, most important, a committed, hardworking, bighearted staff.

Taylor Hall was the first to come on board. By the fall of 2009, Tim was in desperate need of some help. Up to that point, he had been carrying the burden of the campaign virtually alone. He did just about everything, from fund-raising to grassroots organizing to policy to managing the office—and dealing with the media to boot. He used to spend hours on the phone outside our campaign office, pacing back and forth in the field next door, swatting a stick at the weeds and making my campaign run.

The year before, I had met Taylor when he was a brilliant young undergraduate at Furman University in Greenville. He was state chairman of the College Republicans and had invited me to speak at

Furman. He was a smart, tall, skinny kid who left an amazing impression on me. After we announced my candidacy, he sent me an e-mail. He had seen me in a debate and told me he liked that I was the only candidate who talked about fiscal conservatism. Could he help out with the campaign?

"Tim," I said one day that fall, "we need Taylor. That's what we are missing."

By then Tim was used to my coming into the office with new ideas. Sometimes they were off the wall; sometimes they were good. I couldn't tell what he thought of this one.

"Nikki, he's in law school. Law school is not like grad school. You can't just take time off."

I wasn't hearing it. "Tim, we're calling Taylor," I said. "It will be the turning point in our campaign."

Tim was right; Taylor was in law school. Fortunately for us, he was hating it. I think he thought we were a bigger operation than we were, because he was shocked when I personally called him. Tim and I talked to him for two hours.

Tim officially became my campaign manager that fall, and Taylor came on board as deputy campaign manager in January 2010, just a week before he was scheduled to go back to school. From the day he came through the door of our retro little campaign office, Taylor worked like he had been with us from day one. He instantly grasped that Team Haley wasn't about fancy titles and job descriptions; it was about doing what was needed when it was needed.

Taylor did everything from fund-raising to making signs to keeping my schedule. But his real gift was with the grass roots. For months we had been hearing from people who wanted to help the campaign, but we had had no one to coordinate our grassroots support and put them to work. Taylor was that guy. He didn't just organize our grassroots supporters; he motivated them. And he motivated us. Taylor is a man of great faith—he would become known as the "God guy" of the campaign (he led us in prayer before every debate). His faith grounded us and inspired us. I've always said that Taylor was the answer to our prayers. Tim got the help he needed. Our campaign got the jump start it needed. We began to start thinking again that we could win.

The next member of my little dream team started as an intern but got dragooned into working full time. Jeff Taillon will not like my saying this, but he was the puppy of the office. He initially came to us because he needed an internship to fulfill a final requirement to graduate from Clemson. He stayed on after graduation, but his dad gave him an ultimatum: He couldn't work for free anymore and live at home. He had to get a paying job. So one day Jeff asked Tim if he could talk to us later about something. We didn't know what was on his mind at the time, but about fifteen minutes before our talk, Tim found Jeff sitting at his desk, his eyes closed, with "Enter Sandman" by Metallica blaring through his headphones. He was psyching himself up to ask to get paid! Jeff was the office clown—he always kept me laughing. And he grew a lot over the course of the campaign. It was the first time, I think, he had ever really committed himself to something, and he surprised himself with how good he was at it.

Jeff was our jack-of-all-trades, doing whatever job happened to be required on any given day at the office. We didn't have a scheduler, and Jeff filled that position for a while. It became apparent I would need someone else on the job full time when Jeff told a caller I was on Hilton Head instead of in Aiken "because Hilton Head is more important than Aiken." Jeez! We look back on it and laugh now, but Jeff did not have the best phone etiquette.

Rebecca Schimsa was our saving grace. She had just graduated from law school in Charleston and was studying for the bar when we found each other. A group of students at her old law school invited her to come hear me speak. Becca, as we call her, tells me that she wasn't particularly political before then, but after hearing my speech she took a bumper sticker as she left and went out and put it on her car. She says she was impressed with me, but it was really I who was impressed with her. She came in for an interview with Tim and me, and I hired her on the spot.

She asked me about her job description. "Do everything that you think needs to be done, and we'll tell you if you get off track," I said. We never had to tell her.

Like Taylor and Jeff, Becca immediately "got" life on Team Haley. We couldn't afford a phone system that allowed us to transfer calls. So when Becca got a call for the "press department," she would politely ask the caller to hold, put the phone down, maybe answer an e-mail or something, and then walk the phone over to Tim. "I will transfer you to the press department now," she would say as she handed him the phone.

Becca is one of the smartest, sweetest girls I have ever met, but she could also be unbelievably tough. The campaign forced all of us to push ourselves and discover strengths we didn't know we had. Toward the end of the race, when the nastiness broke and the tabloid, trash-chasing press was pursuing us 24/7—literally hiding in bushes and chasing us across parking lots—Becca and Jeff had to step into the role of press wranglers and security guards. With absolutely no prior experience at all, they would scout event locations for me, finding the safest way to enter and exit the building. They herded the members of the press into their designated location and kept them at bay until it was time for me to answer their questions. And they did all this with courtesy and respect. I wish I could say it was always returned.

Along with two interns, Josh Baker and Madison Walker, who we would eventually add to the general election staff, this was my core team. This was my dream team. If any one of them hadn't been there, I honestly don't know that we could have won. They taught me so much about going above and beyond the call of duty. They taught me that people can work toward a common good; spend thousands of hours together; encounter ugliness, betrayal, and selfishness; and come out the other end friends, with their integrity intact. I am blessed that these young ones came to work for me. I hope one day they can look back and feel like they were a part of something great.

We were starting to get excited again. There was just one problem. Mark Sanford was still around, still governor, and still mired in scandal. After the governor's disastrous press conferences following his return from Argentina, the calls for him to resign got louder, but still he refused. All through the early and midsummer of 2009 he hung on. Then in August, after weeks of staying largely quiet and taking a constant beating in the press, Sanford started to fight back.

Keeping the scandal alive were media investigations into the governor's state-funded travel, including the 2008 trade mission during which he saw his mistress. A majority of Republicans in the state senate had called on Governor Sanford to resign. As the summer wore on and allegations about his state-funded travel mounted, the calls for resignation became calls for impeachment. The South Carolina Law Enforcement Division investigated his travel and found that he had broken no laws, but legislators saw it as time to pay Sanford back for all the years they had spent clashing with him. The pressure for him to exit the statehouse in one way or the other—resignation or impeachment—continued to mount.

In August, state senator David Thomas, the Republican chairman of a senate subcommittee tasked with investigating Sanford's travel, charged that the governor had violated the law by flying overseas business class instead of in less expensive seats in coach. State law mandates that, except in special circumstances, all state employees should use the most economic mode of travel possible. Senator

Thomas charged that these revelations were grounds for the house to begin impeachment proceedings against Sanford.

In typical Sanford fashion, the governor fired back by having a press conference outside Senator Thomas's law offices in Greenville. With the traffic whizzing by in the background, he accused his critics of "selective outrage" and produced a letter to Senator Thomas showing that previous administrations had passed up economy class for business and first class at least 230 times since 1984. He accused his opponents of playing politics. "Me hanging up the spurs sixteen months out, as comfortable as that would be, as much as I might like to do that on a personal basis, it is wrong," he said. "One, because as much as you might dislike somebody, it is not right to go and rewrite history."

The governor's press conference was the beginning of a strategy to drag out the mounting legal and political processes against him. And this strategy put me in a difficult place.

I had studied the charges against the governor carefully. I continued to defend him against calls for his impeachment because I didn't believe his actions warranted impeachment. I argued that Governor Sanford had made his intentions clear—he wasn't going to resign. So we might as well get about the people's business rather than play political games.

"Through his own actions, Governor Sanford has become a badly flawed leader, and our state suffers because of it," I said in early September. "But let's not kid ourselves into thinking that his departure from office, and the resulting unchecked power of the general assembly, would make things better. What would make things better is if everyone in the political process started acting like grown-ups, stopped the political posturing and media circus, and got on with the business of the people."

But the shadow the Sanford scandal cast over my campaign continued to hamper my fund-raising and my attempts to break out of fourth place. It was sucking up all the political oxygen in the state. The money people and the press were continuing to write me off. "We killed both in one swoop," opponents of both me and the governor started to say.

The conventional wisdom was that Lieutenant Governor André Bauer had the most to gain from Sanford's leaving before his term was up because he would be able to run as an incumbent in 2010. Lieutenant Governor Bauer seemed to share that view. One of his consultants said to another consultant in an e-mail leaked to the *New York Times*, "I need this guy [Sanford] out," he wrote.

The strategy, though, backfired. The prospect of a Bauer governorship caused people to take a second look at him. Not only had he consistently worked to undermine reformers' efforts to cut spending and streamline government, but he also had had problems with the law. Back in 2003 a police officer had held Bauer at gunpoint after catching him running red lights and going sixty miles an hour in a thirty-five-mile-an-hour zone in downtown Columbia. As the lieutenant governor, Bauer had been issued a warning for speeding when a highway patrol officer recognized him. In another incident, two troopers clocked a state-issued car going over one hundred miles an hour down I-77. As they tried to catch it, a call came over their radio letting them know that the car belonged to the lieutenant governor. The call came from Bauer, using the two-way radio in his car. A review of the lieutenant governor's driving record showed that since 1997 he had had two accidents, four tickets, and one suspended license for not paying a ticket. These run-ins with the law, as well as an incident in 2006 in which he crashed a plane he was piloting, caused South Carolinians to question whether he had the maturity to lead the state.

Meanwhile, my campaign was stalled. Against my better judgment, we tried for a while to get ourselves out of this rut by hunkering down and spending days sitting in an office making calls to potential donors.

But it wasn't working, and it was frustrating. No one knew who we were, and very few people took my candidacy seriously. I knew that if I could get out of the cold-call room and into living rooms, I could win people over. I was sure of that. If could get in front of the voters—even one-on-one, even in small groups—and tell them what I believed and what I wanted for the future of South Carolina, I could change their minds.

In August Tim and I went to a Republican Governors Association candidate-training seminar in Idaho, and someone I respect reinforced what I was thinking. Former Florida governor Jeb Bush gave a talk advising us how to campaign. He said that when he was running for governor of Florida, one of the best things he did was to get out of the campaign office and start talking with people and meeting with people. Just get out and start doing something, he said, anything.

That was all the confirmation I needed. We needed to get out of our brown-walled office and take the power of our voice on the road. So that's what we did. I remembered how I had won my come-from-behind victory for the state house by going door-to-door and talking directly to people. I remembered that I hadn't taken no for an answer when I went into a room looking for help. So I started to talk to anyone who would listen. I accepted every invitation to speak, no matter how small the crowd. And I set two goals for myself. One, I would always win whatever room I spoke to. And two, I would tell that room, "If you like what I have to say, go tell ten people." In the end, this turned out to be one of the keys to our success. I didn't just win over people; I told them I needed their active support. To our surprise, they walked out and e-mailed their lists or told ten people, and then those ten people told ten people, and so on. It didn't happen overnight, but the word of mouth began to grow, at first slowly and then at an amazing speed.

Being with the people turned out to be my favorite part of the campaign. I knew when I started the journey that the only way I would win was if I got the people to care. Care about their wallets, care about their freedom, care about their government. I wanted people to understand the power of their voices—to control their lives and their destinies rather than allow others to control them. If they cared enough to take a chance and speak up for themselves, their families, and their communities, anything was possible. I knew my message was taking hold when I started to hear from people that I had given them hope. What they didn't know then—what I want them to know now—is that I didn't just give them hope; they gave me hope. They gave me the determination to keep going, to fight the establishment, to fight the nastiness, and to fight the belief that underdogs can't win.

I was determined to rebuild the Movement. It had begun under Governor Sanford and, under his leadership and with his motivation, it had made real changes in South Carolina. But when Governor Sanford fell, the Movement fell. When he faltered, everyone and everything associated with him was discredited and written off. It was then that I learned a hard lesson: The Movement couldn't be about one person or one election—it never was. It is bigger than that. It's about government that is accountable to the people. It's about putting taxpayers ahead of special interests. It's about understanding that small businesses are job creators and should be nurtured, not taxed and regulated out of existence.

At every speech I would say that the way to get South Carolina and the country back on track was to get back to basics. Everything went back to spending and the budget. What I learned from my years in business and then my experience in the legislature is that government doesn't understand the value of a dollar the way private businesses do. Government doesn't understand that the money it has comes from the taxpayers—they worked hard to earn it—and it matters how government spends it.

I talked a lot about what government can learn from business. In business the hard times force you to regroup, restructure, and prioritize. Any successful small businesswoman or man knows that the good times will eventually end, and she or he saves for that day. Government doesn't do that unless it's forced to. Unless it's accountable to the people whose money it's spending, government will just keep running up the credit card without any thought of the bills that will come due and who will have to pay them.

I'm an accountant. Numbers tell me stories. So I would reel off what the history of the numbers in the South Carolina budget told me. It was the perfect example of unaccountable government. When I came to the state house in 2005, the South Carolina budget was four billion dollars. The next year is was five billion dollars. By 2007, it was six billion dollars. We had grown government by a billion dollars a year, but no one could really say where it had gone. The people couldn't feel it, and because votes weren't on the record, no one knew who was responsible. And these were our fellow Republicans running up this spending! The reason, I told everyone who would listen, was simple but fundamental: Our politicians had lost sight of what the role of government should be. Government was intended to secure the rights and freedoms of the people—period. It was never intended to be all things to all people. If the people whose money is being spent—the taxpayers—controlled government rather than the other way around, government would live within its means. Like any small business, it would prioritize its spending. When things got tough, it would go through the burn, make the changes needed, and never allow itself to get in that place again.

Requiring that votes be recorded, so that the people would know how the legislators had voted, was one way to make government more accountable. After I began the fight to pass a law requiring votes on the record, the house and senate passed "rule" changes to record some votes. But that was a Band-Aid approach. Rules protect legislators;

laws protect the people. So I campaigned for a law that would put votes on the record—permanently.

Another accountability gospel I preached until I was blue in the face was the need for state and local government to show the taxpayers how their money is being spent through online check registers. These are online databases—Web sites—that provide real-time government spending information to citizens. I knew most South Carolinians were too busy with work and family to go online and check on their government's spending habits, but just knowing the check register was there would keep elected officials on their toes. I compared it to having a teacher in a classroom. If the teacher is around, students behave. If the teacher leaves, the kids cut up, not because they're bad but because they can. Online check registers keep the teacher in the classroom and make legislators more responsible for how they spend.

We also needed to know who our legislators worked for. South Carolina has a part-time legislature. I got paid ten thousand dollars a year to represent the people of Lexington County. Just like everyone else in the legislature, I had to have another job. But members weren't required to disclose whom they worked for in their day jobs. I thought that was wrong. It breeds conflicts of interest. The people deserved to know who paid us. Once they see who is paying their legislators, I said, people will start to understand why policy moves the way it does in Columbia.

Some of my ideas about making the government work for the people again came from my experience in business, some from my experience in the statehouse. One of the things I learned in the legislature was that I am for term limits. I didn't think I was when I came in, but by the time I left, I knew there needed to be a limit on the time politicians can spend in government.

I believe that public officials go to Columbia or Washington, D.C., with the best of intentions. But over the years I served in the legislature, I watched how along the way people with energy and good ideas got broken. They were told not to step out of line. If they did, they might lose their committee assignments and their leadership positions. From business I was used to the idea that you put your most qualified, best people in positions of authority. Government didn't work that way. The people who got the plum assignments in the legislature were the people who had been in line and had gone along with what the leadership told them to do. I didn't think that was right, and I came around to the belief that term limits would fix that. With only a certain amount of time to spend in government, legislators wouldn't have time to play the leadership's games. They would work harder at leaving a legacy of accomplishment and real change for the people rather than at satisfying the leadership.

One idea that I brought from the business world to the state house in Columbia was zero-based budgeting. The year before I ran for governor, I introduced legislation that would inject this simple business principle into state government. The bill required first that every state agency and program go through a comprehensive audit and evaluation. We needed to eliminate duplication, improve efficiency, and phase out programs that didn't work or were no longer needed—just as any business would. The bill also required every agency to adopt zero-based budgeting. Amazingly, state government in South Carolina (not to mention the federal government in Washington) determines its budget each year by starting at a baseline of spending that is "untouchable" and working up from that. My bill required the government to operate more like a business by starting the budget at zero, determining what spending was absolutely necessary, and working up from there. None of the taxpayers' money should ever be "untouchable" when it came to finding savings, I reminded folks on the campaign trail. If that's the case, who's really in charge, the voters or the bureaucrats?

That was my pitch. I always tried to make the issue about something bigger than me, because I always believed it was. I ended each speech by asking people not to vote for me but to join the Movement. I asked them to go tell ten people about it. And slowly, amazingly, they did.

Unaccountable government isn't limited to South Carolina, of course. As my campaign was struggling during the summer of 2009, Americans across the country were coming together to take back their government.

Analysis of the Tea Party—who it is and what it stands for—has become a cottage industry. Some of it, like the false suggestions that members are motivated by racism, is pure politics designed to discredit the movement. But most of the discussion of what the Tea Party means overlooks a basic truth of this country: People have the blessing of freedom of speech. When something is wrong, there is nothing more American than standing up and saying so. That's exactly what the Tea Partiers are doing. They have come together because they think the country is off course and feel the people have lost control of their government. And they want it back.

One of the issues that animated the Tea Party in South Carolina and nationally during my campaign for governor was bailouts. The debate started with the Troubled Asset Relief Program (TARP) passed by Congress in 2008 and signed by President Bush. The TARP bailout was a perfect example of government not understanding the value of a dollar. It was a quick fix to get everyone to calm down. But what did it actually do? The banks that received the money didn't expand lending to businesses. They used the cash to help their own books, and the taxpayers were put on the hook as loan guarantors. No one—not the politicians who encouraged the recklessness, not the quasi-governmental entities like Fannie Mae that got rich off it, and certainly not the Wall Street firms that got bailed out—was ever held accountable. And the American people ended up worse off than they were before. As a small businessperson, I found the message government was sending incredibly offensive. In my version of capitalism, if a company succeeds, you don't punish it by raising its taxes; and if a company fails, you don't reward it by having the taxpayers bail it out.

TARP opened the floodgates for a wave of unaccountable spending that flowed out of Washington. Soon afterward, President Obama bailed out the auto industry to rescue big labor. His allies in Congress passed the $787 billion stimulus bill, most of them without having read it. And he forced through a trillion-dollar health-care takeover. With each bailout, more and more of us felt we were getting further and further from what America was meant to be: a free and striving people with a limited and accountable government. Instead, Washington was revealing itself to be an inside game, with the rules fixed to benefit the establishment. The rules favor the well connected, while the rest of us in flyover country pay the bills.

I've said many times that my goal in public life is to help people find their voices—to control their destinies rather than let others control them; to let people know that they deserve better at all levels of government. In the Tea Party I discovered a group of people who had most definitely found the power of their voices. They were loud and they were proud. We first stood together in the fights against the Obama stimulus bill and for getting votes on the record, and we have been brothers and sisters in arms ever since.

One of the main reasons that the Tea Party and I are such a natural fit is that they understand the importance of putting principles before politics. Critics tried to discredit the Tea Party by calling them stooges of the GOP. In fact, they weren't a party at all. They were Republicans, Democrats, and independents who had had enough and were determined to change things. They instantly understood something that it took me six years in the South Carolina state house to figure out. It wasn't important that South Carolina—or Washington, for that matter—have a *Republican* Congress. What was important was that we have a *conservative* Congress. Big spending and big government weren't working out in Columbia under Republicans any better than they were in Washington, D.C., under Democrats. And unless conservative principles trumped political expediency, that would never change.

Today we're seeing the Tea Party work miracles in Washington, D.C. This energetic and determined group of everyday Americans is running the show in a town headed by Democrats assisted by a hostile, liberal mainstream media. It's no wonder, then, that so many have resorted to calling the Tea Party "extremists" and even "terrorists." The critics are losing the argument—or, in this case, losing control—and all they have left is name-calling. But Americans see this for the desperation that it is.

It's funny. Despite all the success the Tea Party has had in changing the subject in Washington from "How do we spend more of the taxpayers' money?" to "How do we stop digging ourselves into a bottomless pit of debt?" the press continues to ask me if the Tea Party is dying. Wishful thinking, I guess. My response is always "Are you kidding me? We're just getting started!"

I love the Tea Party. They're the reason people are getting energized about their government and elected officials all across the country are getting scared. It's a beautiful thing!

I was working hard in those little rooms, and I could see that I was connecting with people. But it was a strange, quiet time in the campaign. It was too early for the press to pay attention and too early for the voters to be engaged. Nobody was running any ads. The name of the game was fund-raising, and the news for Team Haley continued to be bad on that front.

When the fund-raising numbers came out for that summer, Attorney General McMaster reported raising an astounding $1 million in his first quarter as a candidate. Congressman Barrett had brought in more than $500,000. I had raised a paltry $147,643. That meant that we went into the fall campaign with about $273,000 in cash, while Barrett and McMaster each had more than $1 million in the bank. It was a very tough time for us.

And then, in November, during the Thanksgiving season, came something to be thankful for. Jenny Sanford had moved out of the governor's mansion the summer before and would soon be filing for divorce from her husband, but she never lost her belief in the movement that he had championed. On November 11 she issued a letter to the people of South Carolina endorsing my underfunded, underdog candidacy for governor. She talked about my fight to get votes on the record and what it had cost me. She called me "principled, conservative, tough, and smart." But what meant more to me than anything was that, at a time of very public pain for her, she thought about what was best for South Carolina and looked to me.

"We all know this past year has been very difficult for our state on many levels. It's been hard for me and my family too," she wrote. "But our family is resilient, and we will be fine. And the people of our state are resilient too. I have no doubt South Carolina will get back on its feet. Nikki Haley would be exactly the kind of refreshing, inspiring, energetic, determined governor South Carolina needs to effectively lead our state to a brighter future."

I was nowhere in the polls. I was in fourth place. She didn't have to endorse me—she didn't have to endorse anybody. Nobody would have faulted her for staying quiet and tending to her sons in peace. But Jenny didn't do that. She cared enough about the reform movement she had been so central in starting with her husband that she told everyone I was the best person to see it forward. I'll forever be grateful that she was there for me when so many people weren't.

My father's father, Captain Charan Singh, an officer in the British army in India. I am very proud of my Indian heritage, though I am grateful for the opportunities my parents gave me by moving to America.

I (left) and my siblings Mitti (top), Simmi (right), and Gogi (bottom) took care of each other growing up. Along with my parents, the "original six" was the only family I knew.

The "original six" several years later. All of the siblings are married now with children, but the bonds we shared as the only Indian family in a small Southern town stay with us.

Michael and I on our wedding day. At first my parents had a hard time accepting a non-Indian son-in-law, but once they saw how happy Michael made me, they loved him like a son.

Photo by Renée Ittner McManus / RIMphotography.com

Nalin, Michael, Rena, and I celebrating returns on the night of the South Carolina GOP gubernatorial primary. Running for elected office is a roller coaster ride but keeping my family close throughout helped me stay grounded and remember what really matters.

Photo by Renée Ittner McManus / RIMphotography.com

Celebrating Rena's twelfth birthday the night of the primary. Regardless of the tough business of campaigning and serving my state, I am still a regular mom.

Photo by Reneé Ittner McManus/RIMphotography.com

Me and Nalin in the voting booth during the general election. Seeing my name on the ballot was a powerful moment. Despite all of the challenges growing up and during the campaign, I feel blessed to live in a country that will allow someone like me become the governor of her state.

Photo by Reneé Ittner McManus/RIMphotography.com

My mother, Raj, and I during the primary runoff victory. Watching her and my dad work tirelessly taught me from a very early age that if you truly believe in something, can't is not an option.

Photo by Renée Ittner McManus/RIMphotography.com

Michael and our deputy campaign manager, Taylor Hall, praying with me during the night of the primary. Taylor was key to organizing our grassroots campaign and keeping the rest of the staff grounded and inspired during tough moments.

Photo by Renée Ittner McManus/RIMphotography.com

Rebecca Schimsa and Taylor Hall celebrating primary returns. My campaign staff was—and is—amazing. They made the impossible possible and were there with me for the good and bad moments.

My campaign manager, Tim Pearson, during a rare quiet moment on our tour bus. Our road to victory was a true challenge but Tim pushed through with fierce determination and always forced himself to rise to the occasion. He was key to holding our dream team together and keeping us focused.

Photo by Renée Ittner McManus/RIMphotography.com

Jon Lerner and Tim Pearson watch as I give my inaugural speech. It had been a team effort that led to this moment.

Photo by Renée Ittner McManus/RIMphotography.com

Mitt Romney with me on the campaign bus. The "Join the Movement Bus Tour" was one of the best times of the race — the whole team together, really feeling the energy of the people.

AP Photo / Mary Ann Chastain

Me and Sarah Palin at her endorsement rally in May 2010. Not only did Palin's support boost my campaign, but her advice for me as a fellow wife and mother helped me get through some of the darkest days of the race.

AP Photo / Mary Ann Chastain

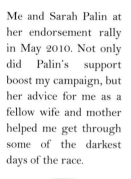

Me with Jenny Sanford after the general election returns came in. Although Jenny suffered an enormous personal tragedy, she never wavered in her devotion to South Carolina and has been a constant source of strength and inspiration for me.

Team Haley celebrating our victory on election night. After some of the toughest months of our lives, this was when we knew it was all worth it.

Governor Sanford and me on the steps of the statehouse right before my inauguration. Despite the betrayal I felt after his personal scandal, I will always admire Governor Sanford's resolve and beliefs about the way the political system should be run. He was the first person to tell me I should run for governor and one of my best mentors.

Me with four former governors of South Carolina: Jim Edwards, David Beasley, Mark Sanford, and Jim Hodges. As the first female, nonwhite leader of my state, I can testify to how much South Carolina has changed since I was a little girl.

Photo by Renée Ittner McManus/RIMphotography.com

My family and me ascending the steps of the statehouse right after I was sworn in. I had fought for the chance to lead my state, and I was excited to start the job.

Photo by Renée Ittner McManus/RIMphotography.com

My in-laws, parents, Michael, the kids, and me in what would become my office. What made Inauguration Day so special was that I got to spend it with my entire family — I never would have gotten there without them.

Photo by Renée Ittner McManus/RIMphotography.com

Chapter Eight
Turning Points

I was the least funded and least known candidate in the GOP race. But throughout the campaign, my team and I sensed opportunity. We knew it was our year.

Henry McMaster led in the polls for most of the race. A former federal prosecutor who had been the state's elected attorney general since 2002, he was the best-known and most liked candidate in the Republican field. Henry is a patriot and a gentleman and had enjoyed a high profile in South Carolina politics for more than two decades. Many observers thought he would be one of two candidates in the run-off that would automatically occur if no one got over 50 percent of the vote. That made the most burning question of the primary who Mc-Master's runoff opponent would be. I knew if it was me, I could win. The challenge was getting to that point.

Gresham Barrett had represented South Carolina's Third Congressional District—in the northwest corner of the state, running from the border with North Carolina south along the Georgia line—since 2003.

The other contender for the runoff was Lieutenant Governor André Bauer. Bauer had been a member of the state house and senate before running successfully for lieutenant governor in 2003. He was a longtime enemy of Governor Sanford and the reform movement. André's advantage was that he had run a statewide campaign—the people of South Carolina knew him. His disadvantage was that more South Carolinians had a negative view of him than a positive one. The result was that Lieutenant Governor Bauer resorted to running what Michael called a "shock and awe" style campaign. He would constantly say outrageous and inflammatory things to get his name in the paper.

I remember watching Bauer in the debates during the campaign. He would carry a sheet of paper with what looked like a list of talking points on it. He would glance at the sheet and then throw out a provocative statement designed to suck up all the media attention in the room. He once compared the government helping the poor to feeding stray animals. "You're facilitating the problem if you give an animal or a person ample food supply," he said. "They will reproduce, especially ones that don't think too much further than that." In another debate he famously blamed illegal immigration on "lazy" South Carolinians who "would rather sit home and do nothing than do these jobs." Then, after throwing off one of his trademark one-liners, he would methodically cross it off the list on his sheet of paper.

As for me, I began 2010 where I'd been all along: in fourth place, both in the polls and in fund-raising. When the campaign-finance disclosures for the last quarter of 2009 came out in January, I had raised less than $560,000. In contrast, Congressman Barrett reported raising more than $2 million. Attorney General McMaster had raised almost $1.5 million. Lieutenant Governor Bauer had raised almost $1.1 million. What these fund-raising totals meant, in real terms, was that each of my three opponents started 2010 with over a million dollars in the bank. I had $406,000.

What could we do? In the true spirit of our campaign, we set out to turn this weakness into a strength. Unlike most of my opponents, South Carolina didn't know me yet. But the rise of the Tea Party and the polling data told us the voters were fed up with the way things were going in Columbia. They were looking for a new direction. I was that new direction. If I could just get my message out, I knew I could win over the state the way I was winning those little rooms.

There was something else we saw in the numbers. Even though no one was running television ads yet, my opponents were already spending freely on the race. Gresham Barrett ran through one million dollars before he put his first ad up on the air. We'd barely spent anything—we didn't have much to spend, and what we did have we were saving for our TV ads. But we began to notice something that confirmed our view of the mood among the voters. Despite all their spending, none of the other candidates' poll numbers were moving much. South Carolinians were holding back. As of March, the Rasmussen poll showed that 29 percent of voters—almost a third of the electorate—were still undecided as to whom they would support in the primary.

We all knew this meant opportunity. South Carolina was looking for something new. The voters were already well acquainted with the attorney general and the lieutenant governor. The candidate who shared my potential for growth with the still-undecided voters was Congressman Barrett. He was well known in his district but was still an unknown quantity statewide. He was well funded and was spending more than anyone else in the race. But he had a vulnerability—a big one for South Carolina in 2010. He had voted for the TARP bailout as a member of Congress in 2008.

While we were having our primary in South Carolina, in Washington, Barack Obama was muscling his trillion-dollar health-care bill through Congress. The more Americans learned about the president's plan, the less they liked it. So the president did what he'd said he wouldn't do and went around the American people. Throughout the winter and early spring of 2010, he and his allies in Congress resorted to backroom deals, and constitutionally suspect tactics to force the bill through Congress. It was everything that was wrong with government on full display: the arrogance of the establishment, the bullying tactics of the feds, and the absolute disregard for the taxpayers who would be paying the bill.

People in South Carolina were outraged by what they were seeing in Washington. For the Tea Party and many others, Obamacare was just one more in a long train of Washington abuses that had begun with the TARP bailout. I shared their outrage. Everything I had fought against in Columbia was happening in Washington, and, what's more, the taxpayers would soon be handed an outrageous bill for it. As far as I was concerned, the health-care law was a part of the same D.C. mentality that had given us the bailouts: Don't fix the problem, just throw it back on the taxpayers and have them pay for it.

We had no money for ads, so we used every other cheap and available means to get our message out. That meant, first and foremost, debates. The South Carolina GOP primary features a punishing debate schedule. In all, we must have participated in about twenty forums with the other candidates over the course of the campaign. That was okay by me. I enjoyed debates and I was good at them. I was determined to use them to remind the voters of Congressman Barrett's vote for the bailout and to make my case as the true fiscal conservative in the race.

The first statewide televised debate was in Charleston at the end of January. Joe Scarborough and Mika Brzezinski of MSNBC's *Morn-*

ing Joe were scheduled to come down on January 28 to moderate the discussion. I was eager for the opportunity to get my message out for the first time to a statewide audience. The major problem for our campaign, however, was that that was the weekend Tim was scheduled to marry his fiancée, Kristin, in Connecticut. We pleaded with the South Carolina Republican Party, which was sponsoring the debate, to move it. They wouldn't. The debate was on Thursday, so Tim ended up flying to Connecticut to prepare for his wedding on Monday, coming back to Columbia for debate prep on Wednesday, going to Charleston for the debate on Thursday, flying back to Connecticut on Friday, and then getting married on Saturday. It was a hectic week for him, but at least it ended well.

Right out of the blocks in the debate, I went after Congressman Barrett and his vote for the TARP bailout. The first question I got, I slammed the congressman for touting his conservatism all across the state but going up to Washington and voting to bail out Wall Street. There was nothing conservative about it. My answer took him by surprise and he fumbled his response. I was feeling good, and then the producers announced that the sound wasn't working on the satellite feed and we'd have to start again. Now he was expecting my attack, but I knew I had to challenge him again on the bailout.

I took a pass on the first question, knowing it didn't make sense to make the same point at the same time. But later in the debate, my opportunity came around again. The moderators asked us which of South Carolina's U.S. senators—Jim DeMint, a conservative who opposed the TARP bailout, or Lindsey Graham, who voted for it—best reflected our political philosophy. When it was Congressman Barrett's turn to answer, he hemmed and hawed and refused to take a position. My turn was next. I said, "Jim DeMint, hands down." Then I turned to Congressman Barrett.

"Congressman, I have to say this. The problem is, Jim DeMint was the only one who voted against the TARP bailout while the rest of you voted for the $800 billion bailout. We don't need that in South Carolina. We don't want it."

Time and again in the debate, I came back to the theme that Washington, D.C., wasn't the answer to South Carolina's problems. I was the only candidate on the stage who had stood firm against taking the Obama stimulus money, and I made sure the audience knew it. Washington was on course to triple the deficit in the first two years of President Obama's administration. It had bailed out Wall Street, bailed out Fannie Mae, bailed out the auto industry, and was on the verge of forcing through a government takeover of health care that Americans didn't want but Americans would be forced to pay for. Washington, I said, was the problem, not the solution.

"There is a new mentality in South Carolina that the stimulus is not good, that a TARP bailout will never help us, and that we can't start relying on the federal government to help us," I said.

Everyone on the stage claimed to be against the stimulus, but they had all agreed that, once it passed, South Carolina should go ahead and take the money. I was the only one who had argued, along with Governor Sanford, that we shouldn't accept it. There were too many strings attached, I had said. South Carolina needed a different approach from bailouts that were hurting private-sector job growth, weakening the dollar, and increasing the debt for our children.

Then Joe Scarborough decided to make it tough for me. Mika Brzezinski had earlier referred to a young girl from Dillon, South Carolina, who had appeared at President Obama's first address to Congress the year before. She attended a 112-year-old school that was in need of repair. "It has just been reported that the Dillon school district is going to get four million dollars in grants and another thirty-six million in loans under the stimulus to rebuild schools there," he said. "Do you support that money? Or should South Carolina send it back?"

Scarborough's question put me between a rock and a hard place. President Obama had used the Dillon school as an example of the good the stimulus package could do when he was trying to sell the bill to Congress. I knew that the politically correct answer was to take the money and run. One politician's pork is another politician's desperately needed "investment," right? Besides that, South Carolina consistently ranked near the bottom of the national educational rankings. Our schools most certainly did need help. But I knew the problem wasn't how much money we spent but how we spent it.

"What I want South Carolina to do is to understand that government is never the answer to the problem. Spending is the problem," I answered. "Right now we spend almost twelve thousand dollars a year to educate a child in this state. It goes through a thousand people at the Department of Education and eighty-five school districts before it ever touches a teacher or a student in the classroom. That's wrong. Less than forty-four cents out of every dollar is going to the classroom."

"So do you want this money, or do you want South Carolina to send it back to Washington?" he asked again.

"I want South Carolina to prioritize and pay attention to how they spend. I do not want any Washington bailout money of any kind whatsoever. It's time that we understand that it's about being conservative, not Republican."

I took a lot of heat for that answer. The next day the local paper called it my "do-over" moment from the campaign. But I believed that accepting stimulus funds would put us in a worse financial position over the long haul, and history has borne me out. The courts eventually ruled that South Carolina had to take the stimulus funds, but it wasn't the free money it was promised to be. The stimulus was supposed to fix our schools and fill the holes on our stretched state budget. But what it's ended up doing is forcing us to start new programs that now need to be funded. It ran up the credit card and gave us more bills to pay, not fewer.

As the campaign went on, I hammered other issues as well, first and foremost jobs. South Carolina had 12 percent unemployment at the time. My mantra was "We can no longer pass government-friendly legislation; we need to pass business-friendly legislation." We needed to take better care of the 95 percent of our economy that was small businesses. I asked voters to put themselves in the shoes of a small-business owner: What would you look for before starting a business in South Carolina? We needed to create a more business-friendly environment, and that started with a good, competitive tax structure.

As an accountant, I could see that we had one of the most complicated, cobbled-together tax systems in the country. The Department of Revenue administered thirty-two taxes, but only three of them were responsible for over 90 percent of the state's revenue. The rest were just adding layers of bureaucracy and killing jobs.

Everywhere I went, I talked about how we needed to look at every single tax, every fee, and every exemption to see how it was affecting jobs. We needed to look, and then we needed to eliminate. The small-business income tax was first on my list. I knew from working in my parents' business that the first thing businesses do when they have cash flow and profit margins isn't to go on vacation but to hire people. The personal income tax also needed to come down to attract investment in South Carolina instead of losing it to Florida, as we usually did. I talked about workers' compensation reform and tort reform to create a business-friendly environment. Boeing was great, I said, but we needed to take care of the businesses we already had, which were overwhelmingly small businesses.

Closely connected to bringing jobs to South Carolina was the quality of our schools. I have two children in South Carolina public schools. How these schools function matters to me in a way that goes way beyond politics. At the time of my campaign, as today, South Carolina was only graduating one of every two high school students in four years. It was and is a disgrace. I had sponsored a proviso passed by the house in March to change the funding formula for our schools to ensure that 70 percent of a school district's per-pupil funding be spent at the school, in the classroom. I advocated for our businesses to get involved in mentoring students in South Carolina high schools. And I talked about school choice. Michael and I had considered lots of schools when we were looking for preschools for Rena and Nalin. We chose the best preschools to match each of their personalities. We had a choice, just as parents help their kids choose a college. If parents help choose preschools and help choose colleges, why don't we have this kind of choice for the years in between—the K–12 years, which really matter? It doesn't make sense. As I told anyone who would listen, my mom used to say that the best thing that could happen for our business was for the competition to move in across the street. Competition provides better service at lower prices. It can do the same in our schools. Then parents, students, and teachers will all win.

Slowly things started to look up. I was getting the attention of the press—for the right reasons. After over two years of battle, the house finally passed and sent to the senate for approval my bill—to permanently require that every vote be on the record. Most important, this was the time during which my dream team was coming together. Taylor had been on board since January, and Becca joined us in March. Things really began to change in the campaign then. We had more organization, more focus. Our non-cookie-cutter campaign didn't start to play by the consultants' rule book, but we did mobilize our grass roots, attract donors, and get our message out more effectively. We began to allow ourselves to think, for the first time, that we could actually win this thing.

Our optimism must have been infectious, because in March, former Massachusetts governor Mitt Romney endorsed our campaign. He weighed in just in time, and it was a great boost for us. The other candidates had already received high-profile national backing. John McCain was supporting McMaster, former Tennessee senator Fred Thompson had endorsed Barrett, and former Arkansas governor Mike Huckabee was backing Bauer. Like Jenny Sanford, Mitt Romney didn't have too much to gain by backing a fourth-place candidate, but he did it anyway.

I have great respect for Governor Romney. He's a true businessman who understands what it means to fix problems. He was brought in during a debt-ridden time for the Salt Lake City Olympics and he turned it around. I endorsed him when he ran for president in 2008 because I strongly believed we needed a businessperson in the White house these last few years.

Many have criticized Governor Romney for his stance on health care in Massachusetts. While I wouldn't choose his plan for South Carolina, I appreciate that he had the courage to try it. I also appreciate his belief that health-care reform is a state's right and shouldn't be a federal mandate. I often think about how different our country would be if Governor Romney were in the White House.

Michael and I feel fortunate to know Mitt and his wife, Ann, and are forever thankful that they came in and endorsed our little campaign when it wasn't popular to do so.

Raising money continued to be a challenge that first part of 2010. This was frustrating to me. I had always been good at fund-raising. Nathan likes to talk about how, when he and I were running for reelection to the state house and making fund-raising calls, he would ask me, "How many people did you call?" And I would say, "Ten." He would say, "How much did you get?" I would (supposedly) say, "I got ten thousand dollars." I would say, "How many people did you call?" And he would say, "Ten." Then I would ask, "How much did you get?" "Sixty-seven fifty."

Nathan exaggerates, but his point is basically correct. My experience had always been that when people knew me and knew my message, they responded. But for the first ten months of my campaign, running statewide for the first time, I just didn't have the name recognition. Too many potential donors wouldn't back me because they didn't think I could win. But if political honchos don't think you can win because you don't have any money, where do you get the money to convince them that you can win?

As I made the rounds looking for support, there were many, many old friends who came through for me. Supporters who had helped me through the years as a legislator in Lexington County were there for me again. There were some new friends as well. The previous summer I had attended a gathering of libertarians and conservatives organized by the Web site RedState.com. My appearance there caught the eye of Erick Erickson and some of the other bloggers at RedState. Their support helped generate financial support from readers across the country. After so many years of trying to get people to understand the power of their voices, it was gratifying to begin to receive the donations—mostly small ones over the Internet, but they made a difference—of people who had already discovered the power of their own. They supported me early and had my back throughout the nastiness of the campaign.

But many of the establishment power brokers—the people who see themselves as the political kingmakers in South Carolina—had a different reaction to me, and I to them. I went to see one old establishment donor who said he would contribute, but only if I agreed to help him with political favors as other candidates had done. Another potential donor wanted me to appoint his wife to a board in exchange for his support. I wasn't interested in playing old-school, quid pro quo games. That was exactly what I was running against. We didn't go back to either of them. I didn't want their money.

Another potential donor I visited after I won the primary was a man with a long history in South Carolina politics named John Rainey. Rainey is a high-profile attorney in Camden who was a longtime friend of Governor Sanford's and a frequent GOP donor. The chairwoman of the South Carolina Republican Party, Karen Floyd, suggested I go see him, so I went. I traveled to his horse farm expecting a pleasant visit and hoping for a fruitful one. Instead, I found myself sitting there in speechless horror as Rainey told me that he could support me, but only if certain conditions were met. He would need to see ten years of tax returns and phone records, he said, as well as have Michael and me undergo full federal background checks. "Why?" I managed to choke out. He explained to me that it would be very embarrassing for South Carolina if I got inaugurated and it turned out that I was related to terrorists. *He did not just say that!* I thought. I left the meeting and called Tim, as mad as I can remember ever having been. "No way," I said. "I don't want his money or his support. He is everything I am fighting against in politics." Rainey, the so-called GOP kingmaker, went on to support my Democratic opponent in the general election. He continues to work hard every day to stymie the reform movement in South Carolina. He reminds me so much of the hate my family faced when I was growing up in South Carolina. His kind of backward thinking is what will continue to hold our state back if it goes unchallenged.

As winter gave way to early spring, though, my fund-raising started to pick up and, as usual, it was the people who responded before the power brokers did. Along with the folks at RedState, at the end of March we launched the Nikki Haley for Governor Moneybomb—a concerted, four-day push to raise fifty thousand dollars online. It wasn't much money to my competitors, but to me it was the world. We cut a fast-paced Moneybomb video that highlighted me as a small-government, fiscally conservative reformer. In it I promised to lead a coalition of conservative governors to push back against the federal government. The response was eye-opening. In just the first day, we raised over $34,000 in small donations from people in South Carolina and across the country. I had an alert on my BlackBerry that let me know when each contribution came in. I drove my campaign staff crazy by announcing each and every donation, no matter where we were or what we were doing.

"Twenty dollars, Corpus Christi, Texas!" I would yell. "Twenty-five dollars, Cleveland! Seventy-five, Harrisburg, PA!"

In the end, over five hundred contributors from forty-six states supported our campaign. Their contributions were small, averaging just over one hundred dollars. But the boost they gave our morale was worth more than the money. We were hearing from people all across the country who wanted to send the message that they didn't care if their politicians were Republican; they cared if they were conservative. They wanted them to be accountable. We knew then, more than ever, that we had the opportunity to make South Carolina a leader in a national reform effort to take back our government.

By the beginning of April, fewer than fifty days out from the primary, finally, slowly, my poll numbers started to move, and the rooms I was working started to get bigger. On April 15—tax day—I spoke to a large crowd gathered on the statehouse steps. It was the second year in a row that the Tea Party had commandeered the statehouse on tax day to fly the flag of freedom. I repeated the line that had become my signature for the Tea Party—"I've never seen people so spirited about their government and elected officials so scared. It's a beautiful thing!" And it was a beautiful thing, seeing all these South Carolinians who didn't care about party and didn't care about race or gender. They just wanted Columbia and Washington, D.C., to feel the power of their voices. I welcomed and cherished the support of the Tea Party movement. I still have never met a more spirited, more committed group of Americans.

The crowds were getting bigger, and the response was enthusiastic. But was it enough to get me across the finish line? Attorney General McMaster had started running television ads the week of the tax day Tea Party rally. Barrett had gone up on the air five weeks earlier. I had reached hundreds of people at the rally, but they were getting their message out to hundreds of thousands of South Carolinians through television. I knew our strategy was to wait as long as we could before starting to spend our precious resources on television, but it was starting to feel like go time needed to come sooner rather than later.

Then, a month to the day before South Carolina Republicans would go to the polls to vote in the primary, all that changed. A nonprofit group with ties to Governor Sanford and associated with the reform movement ReformSC, announced that it had bought $400,000 in television ads. Because ReformSC was associated with Sanford and we had been allies in the reform movement, many expected the ad would boost my candidacy. Tim and I watched it for the first time on ReformSC's Web site the morning it was released. It was a weird experience. Here was the first commercial I had ever been in, and I had had no control over what was in it. Thankfully, its message homed right in on the Movement. It used video from the tax day Tea Party rally to urge support for senate passage of the on-the-record voting bill. I watched myself using my trademark line about the Tea Party—"It's a beautiful thing!"—and then ending, "We've just begun." The ad must have been effective, because later we heard from a woman who told us her young son, after finding out that I had won the morning after the primary, ran to the door of his house, opened it up, and yelled (quoting the ad), "It's a beautiful day for a Tea Party!"

The ad was scheduled to run for two weeks beginning in mid-May, but it ended up running for ten days. My opponents, playing the usual political games, managed to convince a friendly judge to have the ad pulled before it finished its run. They claimed we had coordinated with ReformSC in the release of the ad, which wasn't true. Still, our message had gotten out. I had finally played in the big room of South Carolina politics. Our poll numbers started to move. A private poll taken just two days after the ad began to run showed us gaining on Attorney General McMaster. As of May 12, McMaster was at twenty-four, I was at nineteen, Bauer was at eighteen, and Barrett was at seventeen. Considering that my opponents had been running ads on television for weeks, the statistical dead heat the poll showed me in with Bauer and Barrett was a great sign we were catching on.

Then, on May 13, Tim and I were in the car en route to an event in Charleston. It was the early afternoon and we were late. Tim's phone rang. It was Todd Palin.

"Sarah is going to be in Charlotte tomorrow for the NRA convention," he said. "She wants to come by and endorse Nikki."

Chapter Nine

The Palin Effect

The first thing we needed was an Internet connection.

We were still in shock, and we didn't want to let ourselves get too excited, but we needed to plan, and for that we needed the Internet. So we all headed to Taylor's apartment to process the news Todd Palin had just given us. Taylor had maintained his Charleston apartment after he had come to work for our campaign earlier that year. And Taylor, we knew, had Internet.

Once we got there, we got a little silly for a while. We were all jumping up and down. Governor Palin's endorsement was something that we had been hoping for for a full year, but I had never allowed myself to think about too much because I knew she marched to the beat of her own drum. She did things in her own way and on her own time, and now that she had come through for me, I could barely believe it. We didn't know exactly what was about to happen, but we knew it would be huge for our underdog campaign. Everyone was screaming into cell phones and typing furiously on computers. At one point, Taylor had to make us pause for a group hug. Even Jon was excited.

We didn't have a time for the endorsement, and we didn't have a place, but we couldn't wait to start planning. Governor Palin was scheduled to address the National Rifle Association convention in Charlotte around midday the next day, which would put her in South Carolina that afternoon at the earliest. That meant we had less than twenty-four hours to pull together one of the biggest, if not *the* biggest, events of our campaign. Complicating the scheduling was the fact that Sarah and Todd, in the style they were famous for, were freelancing. They were making plans without the knowledge of their staff, so at first we couldn't get a straight answer about when Governor Palin would be in Columbia. At one point there was word that she would be holding a 10:00 P.M.—yes, 10:00 *P.M.*—press conference!

After we'd had a few minutes to process the news, the first thing Tim did was to impose a campaignwide gag order. No one could tell anyone about the impending endorsement before he could get word to the press, he said. No one could know besides Michael, Jon, Tim, Taylor, and me—no boyfriends, no girlfriends, no parents, nobody. He looked straight at me. "And that includes you, Nikki."

Then Tim got to work on Taylor's computer composing a press release. Taylor got busy putting out a "code red" to our volunteers for people to set up tables, collect e-mail addresses, and sell T-shirts. Tim called Jeff at our campaign headquarters in Columbia and told him to start making "HALEY FOR GOVERNOR" rally signs. "I can't tell you what it's for," Tim told him. "Just start making signs!"

While everyone was busy, I saw my opportunity. I had been warned, but I couldn't help myself. I sneaked outside to the parking lot with my cell phone. Tim, I'm told, looked up from his typing and saw me outside. "Go stop her!" he yelled. Taylor caught me red-handed, with my cell phone to my ear. Sure, I was guilty. But I had a good reason. "It's my mom!" I told Tim pathetically when I got back inside. The endorsement was a big deal. I had to tell my mom. Besides, she wasn't going to run off and leak it to the press. "Okay," he growled reluctantly, and went back to his computer.

Our first challenge was finding a place big enough to hold the crowd we were expecting. I allowed myself to dream: Could five hundred people show up? I would have been thrilled with five hundred people. But where would we put them? There was nowhere indoors that could accommodate both the number of people and the number of press we thought might come. Our best option, we decided, was the statehouse steps, where we'd held the Tea Party rallies, where South Carolinians who wanted their government back were becoming accustomed to gathering.

The other pressing issue I had to deal with was Jenny Sanford. Prior to getting the call from Todd, we had planned on the next day—the day Governor Palin was planning to visit—being Jenny Sanford Day. Jenny had generously offered to do a tour of the seacoast with me, with stops in Charleston, Beaufort County, and Myrtle Beach. I was excited about spending the day with her. Since endorsing my campaign the previous November, she had filed for divorce from her husband and published her memoir, *Staying True*. The commitment she had shown throughout her ordeal had only endeared her more to me and to the people of South Carolina.

Obviously, the event with Governor Palin would disrupt our tour. So now I had to tell this woman who had done so much for me—and had offered to do even more—thanks. . . . I felt terrible having to do it, but once again Jenny Sanford was gracious to a fault. She could have been put out—she had rearranged her schedule to spend the day with me. But she was great. She was happy for us. We were going to go ahead with the first stop on our tour the next morning in Charleston, then fly down to Hilton Head for the second stop, but then, instead of heading up to Myrtle Beach, I was going to have to come back to Columbia. I asked Jenny if she wanted to come with me. "No, go ahead. Tell Sarah I said 'hi!'" she said, and that was it. No complaining, no hard feelings. I've said it before and I'll say it again: Jenny Sanford is the perfect example of strength and grace.

My schedule was clear and we had a location. As soon as we settled on a time—5:30 P.M.—Tim called a political reporter at one of the largest newspapers in the state and gave him the story. He told him he had ten minutes and then he was going to put out the release. By then it was late. We were already exhausted, and we now had less than twenty hours to pull off what would become the most significant event of our campaign. "Can't," as usual, was not an option.

I was like a giddy schoolgirl when Tim and I went out to Columbia Metropolitan Airport to meet Governor Palin the next day. We had never met before, but she and I had an instant rapport. We talked about kids, shoes, suits, and the hard road of the campaign. Immediately we felt a kinship from our shared experiences. So much of what I was going through she had been through already.

We took her to a hotel room across the street from the statehouse where our family and close friends had gathered. She was very friendly and gregarious. She signed books and took pictures with people. There was not one thing about her that was high maintenance. She made a genuine connection with everyone she met.

Meanwhile, the plaza in front of the statehouse was filling with people. My team had worked through the night and pulled off a miracle. The stage was set; there were Nikki Haley signs everywhere. Tim was so busy we had to pull in our policy intern, Josh Baker, an army veteran, father of three, and MBA student, to handle the press. There were more cameras and reporters than I had ever seen at a political event. Josh handled them like a pro, issuing credentials and getting them situated on the risers.

But the real miracle was the people. They came from everywhere. Students drove hours from upstate. Retirees came from Hilton Head. Activists came from Myrtle Beach. Families came from across the state. As we waited for the event to begin, the plaza kept filling and filling. I had hoped that maybe five hundred people would show up. In the end, over fifteen hundred people were there. And all on less than twenty-four hours' notice.

Erick Erickson, a friend who had helped me in so many ways, introduced me. I stepped out onto the statehouse steps and looked out at a sea of people. In addition to our official campaign signs, I also saw homemade signs supporting the troops and the yellow "DON'T TREAD ON ME" flags that have become the unofficial banner of the Tea Party. Across the street you could see people crowded onto balconies and watching through windows. The crowd was pumped up. There was an amazing energy in the air. All I could think of was how blessed I was to have the support of two such amazing women as Jenny Sanford and Sarah Palin. One local paper would later call Jenny and Sarah's support for me "a rock star sisterhood." I couldn't agree more.

"It's pretty cool when you start the day with Jenny Sanford and finish it with Sarah Palin!" I told the crowd. I talked for a little bit, but I didn't want to go on too long. "I get that you are not all here for me," I said. "I get that you might be here for a great friend who has decided to come to South Carolina." Then someone yelled, "We love you, Nikki!" I yelled back, "I'm glad you like me. I love you!"

"She didn't have to do this," I said, preparing to introduce Governor Palin. "She is the one person in this country who has taught every person in this state and this country what it means to use the power of your voice and what it means to understand that government needs to start working for the people again."

The crowd roared. This was Governor Palin's first visit to South Carolina—the McCain campaign had skipped the state in 2008. I stood there with pride and watched the raucous reception she received. She told the cheering crowd she had started her day in Washington, D.C., talking about strong profamily, prolife women candidates at an event for the Susan B. Anthony List, a group of conservative, prolife women. And after that she had gone to Charlotte to talk to Second Amendment supporters at the NRA.

"So I figured, yeah, let me swing by and give a shout-out to a strong, profamily, prolife, pro–Second Amendment, prodevelopment, conservative reformer," she said. "Your next governor, Nikki Haley!"

She was enthusiastic and utterly unflappable. When the few hecklers there tried to disrupt her remarks, she stopped and dealt with them like a pro. "Bless your hearts, protestors," she said. "Keep doing what you're doing, because we have people like Mike and my son in uniform protecting your right to protest, so keep it up, it's cool."

The crowd went wild.

"Stick around," she added. "Maybe you'll learn something."

Then she picked up where our private conversation had left off—in the experiences we shared as wives, mothers, and women in public life. It was amazing how much we had in common. She talked about creating a business-friendly environment in Wasilla when she was mayor, just as I had pledged to do as governor. She talked about how, when she ran for governor, the pundits wrote her off, the establishment ignored her, and the good old boys resisted her. But the people ignored the pundits and the establishment and elected her anyway. She talked about how she vetoed some of the stimulus funds as governor and was overridden by her Republican legislature—eerie! She even said Michael would "make a great first dude in South Carolina"!

Later that night, when Michael, my team, and I finally had the chance to relax at Saluda's, one of my favorite restaurants in Columbia, we looked back in exhaustion at what a successful day it had been. The press was full of accounts of people who had come to the rally undecided or just to see the governor and had come away supporters of my campaign. The momentum we had begun to build with our message of government accountability and taxpayer rights had accelerated. Through the power of Sarah Palin's voice, more and more South Carolinians were beginning to hear my message.

We knew we had to keep our momentum going. On May 18, just four days after the Palin endorsement, we went live with our first television ad. Attorney General McMaster, Congressman Barrett, and Lieutenant Governor Bauer had all been on the air for weeks. But Tim and Jon had wanted to wait until we had enough money to keep our commercials up through the primary. That time had finally arrived.

Like our campaign, our first TV ad was unconventional. While most campaigns would use a biographical spot to introduce the candidate to the voters, we knew we didn't have time for that. We were playing catch-up. South Carolina voters were already familiar with the other candidates, who had been running ads. But the thing was, the people weren't buying what they were hearing. We could see that the competition's poll numbers were flat. We had just three weeks to show them that I was the better choice for South Carolina's future.

So Jon made an ad with just that message. It began with a black-and-white image of Gresham Barrett flashed on the screen: "Bailouts." Then André Bauer: "Stimulus spending." Then Henry McMaster: "Career politician." And then it proclaimed, "South Carolina can do better."

Then the ad pivoted to upbeat music and color footage of me talking to supporters. The tagline called on voters to "Join the Movement."

That was the message we were trying to get across: We could do better. We could do better than the establishment candidates, better than the spend-and-stick-the-taxpayers-with-the-bill mentality that had run Columbia—and Washington, D.C.—for so long. I was a candidate ready to take on business as usual in the state. I was a candidate who was ready to call out Washington, D.C., for piling more debt on the taxpayers. And I was a candidate who was encouraging a movement to reform government, not just promoting myself.

Proof that my ad was needed—as well as proof of the momentum my campaign had gained—came the very day we released it. That night the candidates gathered in Columbia for a televised debate sponsored by the Palmetto Family Council, a profamily South Carolina foundation. The previous Friday, immediately after Governor Palin had praised me for voting against the stimulus, Congressman Barrett had put out a press release calling me "disingenuous and misleading" and claiming that I had voted for the stimulus twice. It was one of those "aha" moments in the campaign. *We must be gaining ground,* I thought, *because the opposition is starting to attack us!*

Asked about those comments that night in the debate, Congressman Barrett repeated his accusation that I had voted for the stimulus. When it was my turn to speak, I set the record straight. The two votes Congressman Barrett was pointing to had not been final—they were votes that didn't result in any bill becoming law. When it had counted—when we had the final vote on the budget that contained the stimulus money—I had voted against it.

"What matters to the people of this state—what matters to the people of this country—is the final vote that affects the people," I said. "My final vote was against the stimulus; it was against the budget that contained the stimulus. Congressman Barrett's final vote was for a Wall Street bailout that had no accountability. You can't deny the facts on that."

Henry McMaster, always the peacemaker, lightened the mood by joking, "I was getting a little scared sitting there between Nikki and

Gresham." The audience chuckled, but I remember wondering if I had entered a new and more dangerous phase of the campaign. Clearly, they were seeing the same thing in the polls that I was seeing. The numbers were moving my way. After months of essentially ignoring me, my opponents were now firing shots at me, and increasingly desperate shots at that. They were trying to portray me as a part of the big-spending, unaccountable establishment that I had spent my entire public life fighting against. It wasn't going to work. And when it failed, what would they try next?

Two days later came the news that sent shock waves through the primary and confirmed what we had been seeing and feeling. The Rasmussen poll showed me for the first time in the lead with 30 percent of those polled. That represented an 18 percent jump from the previous poll in March, when I had been in fourth place with 12 percent. The new poll showed that my next-closest competitor was McMaster at 19 percent; then came Barrett at 17 percent and Bauer at 12 percent.

It was a new race. All of a sudden the "long-shot" Haley campaign was the "come-from-behind" front-runner. All the dynamics had changed. We had worked so hard for so long, and now it seemed like it was finally paying off. But what would have been news to celebrate for most candidates filled me with a sense of foreboding. I flashed back to a conversation I had had with Governor Palin the week before. I was riding with her in the car back to the hotel after our amazing rally at the statehouse. I was pumped up, full of gratitude about her visit, and excited about what it meant. Then she said something that pulled me back down to earth. Her talk turned to the political powers that be and the media, and her tone got serious.

"Be careful. Once they see that you have strength and that you might win, their number one goal is going to be to bring you down," she said, looking at me with a grim look on her face. "And they will never stop."

Chapter Ten
Blood Sport

There was something in the air that Saturday night. We were having yet another debate, this time in Greenville. It was May 22, seventeen days before the primary. The debates were coming twice, sometimes three times a week now. But something was different about this one. Taylor and Becca said later that they noticed a certain "spring in the step" of some of my opponents, a kind of sense of giddy anticipation. What I didn't know then but Tim knew soon after the debate ended was that a rumor was in the air. An ugly rumor. A rumor directed at me.

It was a contentious debate—the most contentious of the race so far. Congressman Barrett started the fireworks by rehashing all his arguments about the ReformSC ad, accusing me of violating campaign finance laws by coordinating with the organization to run the ad. He talked menacingly about "third-party groups" that were "coming into the state and trying to take over South Carolina." I guess he had missed the fact that ReformSC is based in South Carolina and most of its donors are from South Carolina. Still, I defended the fight to get votes on the record, which the ad had advocated. I said I hadn't had anything to do with the ad but sure welcomed the group's support.

After Congressman Barrett attacked me on the ReformSC ad, Lieutenant Governor Bauer did something I had never seen him do before: He too went directly after me. He used the discussion of the ad as an opportunity to attack me for missing the vote when the bill to require voting on the record had been passed in the house a few months earlier.

"With all due respect," he said, directing his remarks to me, "if you're going to push for roll call voting, you ought to be there to vote on it."

I almost laughed. I stood up with a wide grin on my face. Everyone could tell I was gearing up. "You started it!" I joked as I pointed to Bauer. Then I explained how the leadership had deliberately forced through the vote on an afternoon when they knew I wouldn't be there.

Still, I said, "I applaud the general assembly for moving forward to make all its votes on the record."

I had fought for two and a half years to get to that point. "I lost every position I held in the house in this fight to get legislators to vote on the record—long before there was a gubernatorial campaign," I said as I felt my emotions begin to rise. "I'm not going to get caught up in the fact that you're picking on the day that I wasn't there. The two-and-a-half-year fight was the reason that the house overwhelmingly voted to have every single vote on the record."

When the debate was over, I was still a little rattled by the attacks, especially the unexpectedly harsh offense put on by Bauer. I saw Tim huddling briefly with the South Carolina AP reporter. Then Tim, Michael, and I got in the car to drive back to Columbia. On the way we stopped at a restaurant to get some dinner. When we were seated, Tim told Michael and me what he had been talking to the AP reporter about. A blogger who had once worked for Governor Sanford and for me was going to post on his blog Monday morning that he and I had had an affair several years earlier. Tim said the AP reporter had wanted to talk to me after the debate and he wouldn't let him. But the story was coming, he said, and we would have to respond.

Politics in South Carolina has a sad reputation as a blood sport. Our state has been infamous for its last-minute dirty tricks, anonymous phone calls, and personal attacks. It's largely the work of a few consultants and politicians. Everyone knows who they are. But their twisted tactics don't reflect the views of the vast majority of the people of South Carolina, or even most who participate in the political process. The people don't want their elections to turn on scandal; they want them to address the issues that matter to their lives. As Michael and I sat there in shock, struggling to process what we had just heard, I clung to this belief. *The voters will never buy this, will they?* Before I had run for governor, Michael and I had sat down and talked through the worst that my opponents could throw at me. But I had never anticipated this. I had never, ever thought they would stoop this low.

We later learned they'd planned to stoop this low all along. Earlier in the campaign, when I was still very much "Nikki Who," I'd started to get some quiet assistance from the Republican Governors Association (RGA), the political organization charged with electing Republican governors. Refreshingly for a political party committee, the RGA, under the staff leadership of Executive Director Nick Ayers, was willing to be helpful to an underdog candidate whom it thought would be good for the Republican Party rather than being solely focused on who could win.

When word trickled out in the political world that Nick was helping us, he got a call from a leading consultant on André Bauer's campaign. This consultant told Nick—as a professional courtesy—to stay away from me. See, he said, the lieutenant governor's campaign had a blogger in their "back pocket"—someone who, if I ever got any real traction, was going to deal a death blow to my campaign by making outrageous personal claims that no one in South Carolina politics could survive. He was sitting in wait, ready to sling the worst kind of mud if and when I became a real threat in the race for governor. And I had become a threat.

The blogger in question was a sad figure who had been Governor Sanford's spokesman until he was fired. He had pled guilty to criminal domestic violence involving his girlfriend. Against my better judgment—and against the advice of almost everyone I asked—Michael and I had hired him to do some consulting work for me while I worked in the statehouse. We believe everyone deserves a second chance. I had never bought the adage that no good deed goes unpunished, but I started to rethink that faith as Tim told me the details of the smear. All I kept thinking was, *How much would he have had to be paid to do this?*

We continued on our way back to Columbia in a daze and agreed to regroup Sunday morning. The allegation was untrue. It was a transparent political attempt to bring down a surging campaign. It had been less than three days since the poll came out showing me in the lead. Still, we had to respond. The question was how. Michael, Tim, and I got on a conference call with Jon in Washington the next morning and began to discuss our next move. We quickly realized that I had to walk a fine line between staying above the fray and dirtying myself with the ugly details of the charge. Whoever was behind the charge wanted to distract and derail me, and I wasn't going to let them win.

Jon felt it was critical that I be quick and up front in addressing the charges unequivocally. We had been hit hard, he said. We needed to knock down the charge equally hard. The wounds to the people of South Carolina from the Sanford scandal were still raw. The voters needed to be reassured that they weren't going to be the butt of more jokes about adulterers in their statehouse. What's more, Jon argued, I was a young woman, and that made the charge more believable in the eyes of some voters. It was infuriating and unfair, but Jon was right. I thought back to that day almost a year earlier when Tim had told me rumors were swirling around Columbia that I was in Argentina with Governor Sanford. I had been mad then. Now I felt a numbness coming over me. When was this going to end? Was it ever going to end?

We worked up a statement to release when the story went public. It walked the line we needed to walk. It was strong and direct, but it didn't get caught up in the details. My opponents and some in the press would have liked nothing more than for me to put everything else on hold and spend all my time talking about this. But the people of South Carolina deserved better than the dirty politics on which many of the state's establishment political consultants pride themselves.

Tim spent the afternoon on the telephone with the AP writer and editor making the case that the charges weren't true, weren't proven, and didn't merit their coverage. The blogger wasn't a credible person, and he had not a shred of proof, Tim argued. Finally the AP editor agreed to hold off on the story until he saw what was posted on the blog the next morning and checked in again with our campaign. That was all we could do for that day, but we knew the storm was coming. Tim called Taylor, who was in Tennessee for his sister's graduation. "I know I've never done this before," he told Taylor, "but I'm calling a staff meeting for tomorrow morning. You need to get down here." Then Tim called his mom. He told her he felt like he had a dentist appointment the next day. He knew it was going to hurt, but he had to go anyway.

The next morning, as promised, the blogger posted his claims. He said he wouldn't be discussing the matter any further, but that was an assurance virtually no one believed. Tim gathered our little staff at our seventies-style campaign headquarters and told them what was going on. Everyone had been in such a good mood—we were all still coming down off the twin boosts of Sarah Palin and the poll showing us in the lead. Now this. As they heard the news, Team Haley fell silent. Becca and Taylor said later that it was as if someone had died. No one knew what to say. Then someone said quietly, "Is Nikki okay?"

There was some good news that morning. To his credit, the AP reporter called Tim and said he wasn't going to go with the story. CNN called and did the same. *Politico*, an online publication that is widely read in Washington, D.C., and has been known to stir the political pot, also refused to bite. Good for them. The blogger hadn't substantiated any of his claims, and his timing was suspect, to say the least. But the lull in the media storm was only temporary. Late that morning, a local television station became the first outlet to report the allegation. Then the floodgates burst open.

The phone began to ring off the hook at headquarters. While Tim fielded endless media calls, Becca, Taylor, and Jeff were swamped with calls from grassroots supporters, donors, interested citizens, and titillated strangers wanting to know if the allegations were true. Overwhelmingly, the South Carolinians we heard from were outraged by the charges. They were embarrassed to be going down this road again. Many were asking what they could do to help us fight it. Others said it only made them support me more. As the story spread, calls started coming in from throughout the country. We even heard from Taylor's grandmother, a Southern Baptist lady in her eighties who lives in Tennessee. "I don't even care if it's true," she said. "I don't like the way they're treating her. It's not right."

But if the people weren't playing along with the politics, the press was a different story. After showing some initial restraint, they lost all control. The media began to camp out in front of campaign headquarters, actually attempting to peer through the blinds as my staff was working inside. One Columbia network affiliate even went to my house to try to interview Michael and the kids. The situation was rapidly spinning out of control. We put out the statement we had worked up the day before in an attempt to contain some of the chaos:

> I have been 100% faithful to my husband throughout our 13 years of marriage. This claim against me is categorically and totally false.
>
> It is sad, but not surprising, that this disgraceful smear has taken form less than a week removed from the release of a poll showing our campaign with a significant lead. It is quite simply South Carolina politics at its worst.
>
> These attacks—and those sure to follow—are an effort at distraction, but I will keep my focus on what matters, and that is delivering South Carolina's government back to our people. That's a fight I have fought for the last five years. That's why I entered this race for governor. And that's what I will continue to do, despite any outrageous and false claims that are thrown at me.

While that statement satisfied most citizens, it did not quench the media's thirst for tabloid politics. That night there was a debate scheduled in Greenville sponsored by the chamber of commerce. We had a decision to make. We knew massive amounts of press would be there, and I knew I didn't want to run from them. They had a job to do. I had answers I wanted to give.

As the initial shock of the accusation wore off, I actually began to gain strength from the mudslinging. All my old instincts to fight through the adversity, to prove myself to the skeptics and the critics, started to come alive. While some were using this as a chance to destroy me and my family, I would use it to strengthen myself and protect my family. I went on the radio that day and started talking to the people through the press, letting them know that we knew this was a distraction by my opponents to knock me off message. What my opponents didn't realize was that these attacks only made me more determined. Politics can be an art of distraction. Elections can be made to be not about issues but about throwing the other candidates off. That was the game some politicos in South Carolina liked to play, but it wasn't mine. I didn't have to play it and I wouldn't.

God bless my team. In a matter of hours, Becca, Jeff, and Taylor had to transform themselves from mild-mannered campaign staff into a combination of Secret Service agents, bodyguards, and press wranglers. The Greenville debate set the pattern for the remaining events of the primary. We had no security staff for the campaign, so the team had to be my security. Becca and Jeff arrived at the debate site, a huge convention center in Greenville, two hours before start time. Their job was to figure out safe routes in and out of the building. The front door was no longer an option for me.

As we expected, when I got there, the media contingent in front of the convention center was huge. Michael was driving, and he got us in the building through the designated back entrance. So far, so good. But as I was in the ladies' room getting my hair and makeup done for the debate, a female reporter came barging through the door. Michael, who was standing just outside the door with Tim, saw the reporter make her move. He intercepted her and had to physically block her from entering the ladies' room. When I was done, we tried to make our way to the candidate holding room adjacent to the stage. A gaggle of reporters and cameras began to chase us down the hallways toward the stage. When we got to the stage, we passed a stand of curtains. Michael kicked the stand out from under the curtains as we passed, and the whole thing came falling down on the pack of paparazzi. It was like something out of a movie. Except it wasn't a movie. This was my campaign, and it was literally under siege.

In the debate, I once again denied the allegations. "If anything, I am more focused and motivated than I have ever been to run in this race," I told the business crowd. I also challenged the other candidates to denounce any and all smear tactics. McMaster and Barrett promptly agreed. (Henry later told his staff that even talking about the charges was a fireable offense.) Lieutenant Governor Bauer was not on the stage.

I had planned to meet with the press in an organized fashion after the debate, and I did. I couldn't believe what I was facing. In a matter of days, I had gone from no one caring about my campaign to having a pack of salivating wolves following me everywhere. Still, I wasn't going to play the game. I wasn't going to be distracted. I answered their questions about the scandal and returned to my message about bringing open, accountable, and effective government to South Carolina.

I had a breakfast meeting scheduled with a group of women business owners the next morning at the same location, so Tim, Becca, and I stayed overnight in Greenville. The next morning Becca was doing her Secret Service/advance routine at the meeting location, scouting the safest routes in and out, when she was approached by a reporter with a camera crew from the Greenville Fox affiliate. They hadn't been at the press conference the night before and seemed desperate to get me on camera talking about the charges. Becca told them she wasn't a press person and tried to wave them off. When their camera was ejected from the private breakfast meeting, that seemed to make them even more angry. They refused to leave. As I left the convention center after the meeting, the camera crew was still there. I watched in amazement as they literally sprinted across the parking lot and down the driveway after my car!

Becca, who was taking her own car back to Columbia, watched what was happening and wisely stayed inside the convention center until she felt it was safe to leave. As she walked outside to her car, the

Fox reporter approached her, yelling, "Why didn't we get to talk to her!" Holding a box of T-shirts, Becca repeated that she was not the press person. They should call the office. Then the cameraman put the camera in her face. "What's your name!" screamed the reporter. "Don't you have a name?!"

"I do," she said, "but I'm not telling you." Then she put down her box of T-shirts and ran back into the convention center, crying. The security guards had to go out and move her car into the garage so she could leave the back way. Tim called the news director at the station and bawled him out. It was not the press's finest hour.

I had no other choice: I went into survival mode. The press hounded us everywhere, refusing to talk about anything but scandal. The funny thing is that the attacks only sharpened our focus and strengthened our determination. We quit reading the newspapers. We turned off the television. We hunkered down and worked even harder. Michael took a leave of absence from the army and joined the campaign full time. I was deeply reassured by his constant presence on the trail, and both of us felt great comfort in knowing that Rena and Nalin were being taken care of by my parents and sister. The kids didn't know the details of what was wrong, but they knew something was wrong. I figured the best way to let them know everything was going to be okay was to hug them and kiss them. So that's what we did.

It was a defining moment in the campaign. We knew then we were in a bigger fight than we could ever have imagined. This was no longer about winning an election. This was about defending our family, defending our reputations, and defending what was right against everything that was wrong with South Carolina politics. We had been attacked mercilessly, and we weren't going to let them win. They could beat us on money, they could beat us on name recognition, but they weren't going to beat us with hate and lies.

I found myself determined to fight through it but also sad about the toll it was taking. We had all worked so hard for twelve months. I was disgusted by the people involved and the lengths they seemed willing to go.

I worried about my staff too. Tim, Taylor, Becca, and Jeff had put so much energy into the campaign. They were trying to take care of me, but I knew this was the time I needed to take care of them. I was angry, but I tried not to show it. I stayed strong in front of the press and in front of the haters. My staff, I thought, needed to see that I could handle this. In the end, all the ugliness made us even stronger as a team. We got closer. The already incredibly tight bond we felt grew even tighter. Still, at the time, I thought I needed to put on a brave face. I saved my moments of disappointment and sadness for when I got home. In those moments, alone with Michael, all the emotion of the day would come rushing out. I will always look back on that time and know it was Michael who got me through it.

For a while, politically, it felt a lot like the days after the Sanford implosion. Friends we thought would be there for us were absent. There were exceptions, of course, and different friends dealt with the news in different ways. Sarah Palin called me from Wasilla the day the smear went public. She asked me two questions: "Are you okay?" and "Is it true?" I answered "yes" and "no." "Then fight," she said, and she promised she would help. A little while later, Tim was on the phone with Todd and heard Sarah in the background typing and yelling, "Tell them it's coming, Todd!" Within minutes, she had a Facebook post up defending me. She titled it, "Nikki Haley in Opposition's Crosshairs: A Good Sign for Nikki and South Carolina!" She was tough, supportive, and defiant—everything we love about Sarah.

"When Nikki and I held her endorsement rally on the steps of the beautiful and historic South Carolina state house a few weeks ago," she wrote, "I warned her and her family that she would be targeted because she's a threat to a corrupt political machine, and she would be put through some hell. That, unfortunately, is the nature of the beast in politics today—especially for conservative 'underdog' candidates who surge in the polls and threaten to shake things up so government can be put back on the side of the people."

Sarah goes with her gut, and I love her for that. But different strokes for different folks. Jon got a call the day the news broke from an aide of another supporter, Mitt Romney. Mitt's team told him that they were going to have a "Nikki Haley meeting" the next morning to decide what to do next. Mitt ended up being very generous in his support of me, for which I am very grateful. But the differences in the way the two people reacted reflected the differences between a brash, spontaneous Alaskan woman and a cautious, deliberate businessman. However they came to it, I was thankful for their support.

Unsurprisingly, the blogger reneged on his initial statement that he would not comment further on the matter. To keep the story alive and the attention focused on him, all through that week he dripped out one unconvincing detail after another. He repeatedly promised to present proof of the affair and repeatedly failed to do so. Tim and Jon settled into a grim routine in which Jon would call Tim at his home each morning around 7:00 A.M. to ask, "What did that moron put up today?" Tim and Jon would come up with a statement by Tim to address the latest charge. I told them to handle it. I refused to get dragged down into the mud and stayed focused on our message of jobs, education, and accountability. The legislature was still in session, so I spent much of my day at the statehouse. If Tim and I needed to talk, we would text each other to meet in the back stairwell off the house chamber.

The media's interest in the story was obsessive, not just in South Carolina but across the country and even overseas. The Indian press, the British press—all kinds of media that had never been interested in a South Carolina governor's race before were suddenly covering the story. Still, we did our best to stay on message, to not play the game. The day after the story broke we released a new TV ad—our second— featuring footage from the Palin rally.

As the chaos continued, the reality was that we had campaigning to do. I couldn't control what the press did, but I could control what I did. So I did what I loved the most: I got out with the people. We scheduled campaign stops and I kept them. But I couldn't help but worry: Would people show up? What would they ask? Would they leave us?

One campaign stop that first week after the nastiness broke went a long way toward answering my fears. It was a candidates' forum in Greenville. Before I went out onto the porch of the restaurant where the event was being held, I took a deep breath and thought, *Nikki, the press doesn't define you—how you handle this will.* I walked out, and a candidate for lieutenant governor was speaking. The crowd immediately turned to look at me. Then, one by one, they stood up and started applauding. Their applause got louder and then turned into cheers. The speaker couldn't make himself heard over the commotion and stopped. The crowd whistled and cheered and I heard someone yell, "We know the power of our voice, and we want the press to hear that we love you!"

When people ask me what's the moment I remember most from the campaign, it's that one. After all the hate, the people didn't leave me. Not only that, they showed the power of their voice to fight for me. They strengthened me that day. They inspired me in a way that they will never know. At that moment, I remembered why I was doing what I was doing. It was for those people that I would fight.

I was in the car with Tim and Michael, as usual, when the second shoe dropped. It was June 1, seven days from the primary. We were headed to a debate at Francis Marion University in Florence when Tim's phone rang. I heard silence from Tim for a while, then he said, "You know he works for André Bauer, don't you?" Then more silence. Then he hung up.

Tim gave me a look that told me he didn't have good news. The call was from a reporter from Greenville. The reporter had just gotten off the phone with a well-known lobbyist in Columbia. The lobbyist was alleging that he had had a one-night stand with me on a trip to Salt Lake City in 2008. The reporter was asking if the allegation was true. *What? You've got to be kidding!* I couldn't believe that it was happening again—and this time from a campaign consultant of my opponent! It was the second smear in as many weeks. Once again, I was being forced into the humiliating position of having to deny being unfaithful to my husband. It was a lie, it was ugly, it was sexist, and it was crowding out all of the issues the people really cared about in the campaign. Again I found myself wondering: *How much are these guys getting paid?*

We were headed to a debate in Florence. I was numb. After it was over, everyone said I had done fine. But I was on autopilot. I'll take their word for it. Tim spent most of the car ride from Florence to Columbia talking to the reporter from Greenville and once again arguing that the charge didn't rise to the level of news. The lobbyist was admitting that he had no proof of what he was saying. What's more, Tim repeated, he was on the payroll of a rival campaign! Tim did his usual persuasive, fantastic job. Still, he hung up not sure what the reporter would do. But by that point, quite frankly, none of us had any idea what the press would do next. We had given up on the press's attempting to bring any credibility to their process of reporting the "news."

We woke up the next morning expecting another ugly story to be splashed across the front pages. But there wasn't one. *Good for them,* I thought. *They're not playing the game.* Then something interesting happened. The Bauer campaign sent out a press release saying it had fired the lobbyist, who had been its paid consultant up until that day. Tim talked later to a reporter about the press release and the reporter asked, "Why are they doing this?" Tim said, "I don't know, but have you ever heard of a campaign sending out a press release when they fire a consultant? It just doesn't happen." The reporter repeated his question. "So why are they doing it?" Tim was as tired of the scandal and the dirty tactics as I was—maybe more so, because he had to spend all day dealing with reporters who couldn't seem to get enough of the nasty details. So he vented and used words both of us were grateful never found their way into a newspaper. "She kicked their ass on policy, so now they're calling her a whore," he said in exasperation.

There was yet another debate that night in Charleston. It was being carried live. For this debate we were all lined up behind a single, large podium on the stage. As we waited for the questioning to start, I saw Bauer and Barrett talking to each other and laughing. Then, just as the lights came down and the cameras started to roll, I looked over and saw the two men high-five under the table. They actually high-fived!

I had been pretty calm up to that point, but seeing that made me angry. For the first time I really questioned whether it was all worth it. I hated the game that was being played.

The first question out of the box was about the lobbyist's accusation. The moderator asked me to respond to the attacks. I was angry and I was determined, not just to fight back against the lie but to fight back against the dangerous motives behind it.

"For the last six years I have been fighting the establishment for the good of the people. They are now fighting back," I said. "This is disgusting politics. I was—two, three months ago—Nikki who? No one was saying anything. Then we started going up in the polls, and now we have had everything thrown at us."

The moderator, Charleston channel 5's Bill Sharpe, then turned to Bauer and asked him what he knew about the charges. After looking like a deer in the headlights for a few seconds, Bauer admitted that the lobbyist had worked for him but insisted he knew nothing else and wasn't going to comment on it.

That was too much for me. I turned on Bauer. "But Lieutenant Governor, you paid him. He was a paid consultant for you."

"And when I found out that there may be things that could possibly be true or could not be true, I didn't want to associate with that type of behavior, and so I ended the relationship," Bauer said.

I thought back to the call from the reporter that Tim had received the day before. "But you were fishing the story last night, and you didn't fire him yesterday," I countered. "It was only when no one would take it seriously because he is a paid consultant that you decided to fire him today."

Bauer didn't have a response to that, but I didn't really care. I had tried to run a good and respectful campaign. I had tried to run a campaign on the issues. All I could think of was how mad the voters of South Carolina must be. Here we were, trying to decide who would lead their state for the next four years—who would get their husbands and neighbors back to work, make sure their kids graduated from high school and fight against going deeper into debt with Washington, D.C.—and all we had talked about for the past two weeks was accusations and hate. I couldn't stand it. I couldn't stand that it was taking something that I thought was so high—leading the people of the state that I loved—and bringing it so low.

"I think this is sick politics," I said. "It reeks of everything that's wrong with the establishment. It reeks of everything that is wrong with South Carolina politics, and I will fight it every step of the way because South Carolina people are done with this. We are done with the dirty politics that are giving this state a bad name."

I just wanted it to be over. There had been so many lies and so many destructive games had been played. I was so tired of it. I wanted to get out from behind that podium, get off that stage, and punch those guys. Then I just wanted to go home with Michael and Rena and Nalin.

When I saw Michael, Tim, and Taylor after the debate, I said, "You'll never believe what I just saw." And I told them. "They high-fived!" All we could do was shake our heads in disbelief. *Six days,* I thought. *Six days and it will all be over.*

That Friday, June 4, an Associated Press story on my campaign began like this: "A GOP lawmaker hoping to be the state's first female governor is getting publicity for all the wrong reasons." First, there had been the blogger's accusations, the story read, then the lobbyist's, and now this.

The previous day, on an Internet political talk show called *Pub Politics,* in which a Democrat and a Republican drink beer and talk politics, state senator Jake Knotts, a Bauer supporter, had said: "We've got a raghead in Washington. We don't need a raghead in the state-house."

Here we go again, I thought. You couldn't make this stuff up. It was getting beyond ridiculous.

Jake Knotts is a self-described "redneck" with a reputation for . . . let's just say "blunt" language. As far as I was concerned, he was the poster boy for everything that is wrong with South Carolina politics. When I heard what he had said, I was immediately angry because I knew his comments would go national. They would be repeated by media all over the country and the world. At a time when I wanted people to feel good about our state, he was an example of why we've been regarded as a bunch of uneducated, backwoods racists. So I re-fused to dwell on the ignorance of one senator. The press once again hounded me to respond, and I just said Knotts's comments were unfortunate and didn't represent the people of South Carolina. That was the saddest, most regrettable thing about the senator's bigoted remark: Jake Knotts doesn't reflect the views of most South Carolinians, but here he was, reinforcing everyone's worst stereotypes and prejudices about our state. It was so unfortunate and embarrassing.

The previous weekend, Michael, the kids, my little campaign staff, and I had gone to a supporter's house in Myrtle Beach. We were beyond exhausted, physically and mentally. We spent two days in that house. We never left, except to go to the grocery store. We grilled and cooked pasta. Taylor slept. And Jon and his crew came in and we filmed an ad that I think was one of our best of the campaign. It would go on to be recognized by the *Washington Post* as one of the best in the country in 2010.

Throughout the campaign I had clung to this faith that God wouldn't let bad win in this election. I'm not saying I thought He wanted me to be governor. But I couldn't believe—I didn't believe— that He would let the sleaziest and most bigoted elements of our state's politics win. I had that faith. It kept being tested, but I clung to it. All the bad that these people had tried to do to me would come back and expose them for how awful they were. They would lose. Right would win.

Our new ad went on the air the day before state senator Knotts's remark. Looking back, the timing was fortuitous. The ad reflected my faith that God wouldn't let bad win, even as Knotts was piling on with his hate. It opened with thunderclouds as I said, "I have seen the dark side of our state's politics." Then I continued with "And I know the bright side of our state's people" as the ad cut to images of Michael, the kids, and me on the beach and a man tossing his little girl playfully in the air.

The irony is that, for those who orchestrated the smear tactics, the mudslinging backfired in more ways than one. In the last two weeks of the campaign, no one—not me, not Congressman Barrett, not Lieutenant Governor Bauer, and not Attorney General McMaster—could get their message out. It was all scandal, all the time. If someone thought they could distract me by throwing dirt at me, all they did was distract everyone else.

In the end, the smear tactics backfired in the most important way of all: in revealing the true character of the people of South Carolina. The best thing—the only good thing, really—about those last days of the campaign was the people. The political machine was showing its ugliest side. It was throwing everything at me it possibly could. But the people saw through it. They were smarter, better, and ultimately stronger than the political machine. In the end my faith was rewarded by the people of South Carolina. I continue to be in awe of their goodness and the goodness of Americans from across the country.

We had done our own polling and knew roughly where the race was going into primary day. But with so much junk swirling around the race, we couldn't know for sure what voters were thinking or believing. Jon felt confident that we would come in first but was equally confident that we would not hit the 50 percent needed to avoid a runoff.

I kept saying it over and over: "Fifty plus." That's what we needed—anything over 50 percent of the vote—to avoid a runoff. It had been such an exhausting year, topped off by the final, brutal last two weeks of the campaign. And we had come so far. If you had told me just four weeks earlier that on primary night I would be hoping to avoid a runoff—instead of praying to make it into one—I would have said you were crazy.

But here we were. I was done. My family was done. My campaign staff was done. I couldn't bear the thought of another two weeks of battling for the nomination. Considering what we'd just been through, I didn't even want to think about what the political machine might crank out to try to destroy me in a runoff. The thought of it literally made me sick to my stomach.

The party room was my getaway. It was full of family and Rena's friends. We sang "Happy Birthday," and as she blew out the candles, Rena looked at me and smiled. I knew why she smiled. I knew what she was wishing for. There were so many blessings in my life. Two of the sweetest for me and Michael are our two children. They are loving and caring, funny and playful. But most important, they are ours.

After the party was over, Michael and I stayed in the war room, where Tim, Taylor, and Becca were huddled monitoring the returns coming in. Jon joined us by phone. As we got closer and closer to 50 percent, I repeated my mantra: "Fifty plus! Fifty plus!" Jon replied with his usual blunt honesty: "Don't say that, because it's not going to happen."

Boy, was he going to look silly. The polls closed at 7:00 P.M. By just after 9:00 P.M., with 54 percent of the precincts reporting, I was in the lead with more than 47 percent of the vote. Ten minutes later, with 65 percent of the precincts reporting, my lead had crept up to over 48 percent. So close! It was excruciating. My closest competition, Congressman Barrett, was way back in the low twenties. I should have been happy. Instead, I was in agony. I kept turning to Tim and berating him, "We need less than one percent—*less than one percent!* What about the absentees? Have they counted the absentees?" Tim looked at me patiently. "It's not coming, Nikki. You're going to have to be happy with just under fifty percent," he said. "And by the way—that's a very cool thing! We were nowhere and we crushed the competition."

At 9:47 P.M., the AP projected that I wouldn't pass the 50 percent mark to avoid the runoff. With 87 percent of the precincts reporting, I had 48.9 percent of the vote. When all the precincts had reported, I had a maddening 49.5 percent.

I retreated to the ladies' room. I knew I should be happy that I'd gotten 49.5 percent, rather than sad that I hadn't gotten 50 percent, but I couldn't help it. Yes, it had been a four-way race with serious competitors. And yes, we had exceeded all conceivable expectations. But my goal was to win—not to almost win. Not to get the chance to try again to win. To win.

After I'd been in the ladies' room for a while, my mom came in to check on me. Then my dear friend Eleanor Kitzman came in. Eventually Tim was in there as well. The reception room was packed with people waiting for me to speak to them, he said. These were the people who had made it all happen for us. They were people to whom we owed so much. I needed to get out there. But I didn't know if I could do it. I was just so exhausted. How do you go face the people who helped you get so close when there's a part of you that doesn't know if you've got two more weeks in you to finish the job?

Tim wasn't hearing any of it. This is a good thing, he kept reminding me. It doesn't matter if we have to go to a runoff. We won—we won bigger than we ever dreamed we would. He even turned my signature catchphrase back at me: "It's time to get excited about it."

For the first time in the campaign, I had to struggle to rally and put on my game face. But I got it together, gathered Michael and the kids around me, and went out to face the crowd. As soon as we walked onstage, all my exhaustion and my misgivings left me. My entire family was there. There were more national media than we'd ever seen before in the campaign. And the crowd was amazing. From the back of the room, a chant began and grew louder until it engulfed the whole space. "Nikki! Nikki! Nikki!"

"From the very beginning, it was us versus the establishment," I said when they finally quieted down. "But we had something they didn't have. We had you."

The crowd exploded in screams and applause. I started to feel good. All my regret at not winning big enough was being replaced with gratitude for all we had accomplished. I ended my brief speech the same way I had ended almost every speech, debate, and rally of the campaign.

"I am a woman who understands that through the grace of God all things are possible."

"I am the daughter of immigrant parents who reminded me every day how blessed we were to live in this country."

"I am the sister of a man who fought in Desert Storm, and I still remember what it was like when we didn't know if he was coming home." (At which point my brother Mitti bellowed, "Hooah!")

"I am the sister of a family who, when all this got dirty, all they did was say, 'We love you. You fight. We're here for you.' "

"But I have to tell you this," I concluded, barely able to keep it together. "I am the wife of a man who puts on a military uniform every day." I pointed to Michael and the kids standing behind me. "This is what has kept me strong every day for the last two weeks."

I meant every word.

The questions about whether Congressman Barrett would—or should—drop out began before the final vote was tallied. At around nine thirty on election night, the *Washington Post*'s Chris Cillizza tweeted, "Question for Gresham Barrett: If Nikki Haley is just short of 50% . . . does he stay in the race?"

In the final vote tally, I received 49 percent of the vote, Barrett got 22 percent, McMaster 17 percent, and Bauer 12 percent. Given the twenty-seven-point spread between us, there was pressure, not just in Washington but in Columbia as well, for Barrett to stand down and not contest the race. The Democrat one of us would face in November, state senator Vincent Sheheen, had won his nomination outright. He hadn't wasted any time declaring that the general election began on primary night. Some wondered what could be gained by dragging out the GOP nomination while Sheheen got a two-week head start. But Congressman Barrett continued in the race, as was his right to do.

More than once during the campaign I said that Attorney General McMaster was the candidate I started out knowing the least and by the end of the primary became the one that I respected the most. Henry was a true gentleman throughout the campaign. He didn't engage in the smear tactics that the other campaigns stooped to. He was funny, and he loved the state of South Carolina. He genuinely wanted people to be proud of our state.

I wanted to ask Henry for his endorsement immediately after the primary, but I hesitated. Michael and I felt for him. I couldn't imagine going through everything we had just gone through and not making it to the runoff. I struggled with calling Henry, knowing that he and his wife, Miss Peggy, would be hurting from the loss. Finally, a couple days after the primary, I worked up the courage to call. "I just want you to know I respect your fight," I told him. "I hope you'll take some time and allow yourself to get away and breathe." I wasn't going to ask him for his support then. I knew if the tables were turned I would want time. I told him that I would call the next week.

In the meantime, there was campaigning to do. The idea of doing a bus tour had always appealed to me, so we rented a passenger tour bus and prepared to launch the "Join the Movement" tour. The idea was to put the campaign on the road and take our message to South Carolinians. My dream-team staff came along. Michael was with me too. We didn't know what to expect from the runoff so, fearing the worst, we sent Rena and Nalin to stay with my brother Mitti and his wife, Sonya, in Atlanta. But later they joined us on the bus. We were thrilled to have Jenny Sanford and Mitt and Ann Romney join us for a few stops as well.

After a week had passed and we were ready to launch the bus tour, I called Henry and told him I would appreciate his support. Not only did he give it, but he became one of my biggest cheerleaders. Tim sent him the schedule of the tour and told him that whenever he could join us, we'd love to have him. He replied that he was in for every stop, and he was true to his word. He did the whole tour with us.

Everyone fell in love with Henry on the bus. The crowds we attracted as we traveled up and down the state and along the coast were big and boisterous. Henry clearly loved all the people and the excitement. He would spend hours with me, shaking hands and taking pictures, his love for the state of South Carolina shining through.

Music, as usual, was a big part of the tour. Henry is a musician, and he shares my love of rock and roll. Just before I was inaugurated as governor, Henry and Peggy had Michael, the staff, and me over for dinner. We ended up in a jam session, with Henry on guitar and harmonica, me on the tambourine, one of the security detail on drums, and Michael and Tim singing. I think there is more than one of us who is grateful the session wasn't recorded. When we pulled up to an event on the bus tour, we would blast some Black Eyed Peas or Tom Petty. Henry would introduce me as if I were headlining Lollapalooza. "As the poet Tom Petty says," he would say, with his voice rising to a dramatic pitch, "You can stand her up at the gates of hell and SHE WON'T BACK DOWN!"

Sometimes he was a little more philosophical. "As the poet Bob Dylan says, the times they are a changin'. Ladies and gentlemen, Nikki Haley!"

For the first time in a long time, campaigning was fun again on the bus tour. For that I am thankful to Henry. He selflessly endorsed me and asked for absolutely nothing in return. Not only that, but we gained two talented and experienced staff from his campaign. Trey Walker had been his campaign manager and later joined our team as deputy chief of staff. Rob Godfrey, who had been Henry's communications director, joined Team Haley as our press secretary.

Elections and opponents can be very hateful, but Henry is that bright side of South Carolina that I know and love. Michael and I are blessed to have met and become friends with Henry and Peggy McMaster. Not only did Henry support me during the runoff, but his support continued throughout the general election. He and Peggy remain trusted and respected friends. I hope we can continue to gain strength from their love for South Carolina and learn from their graciousness. They showed my family true generosity at a time of great pain for their family. For that we will always be grateful.

After the runoff, the real campaign began again. I was the Republican nominee. I had expanded my primary lead and won 65 percent of the vote to Barrett's 35 percent. For the second time in two weeks, I got majorities in forty-two out of forty-six South Carolina counties.

It was a big night for me, but it was a bigger night for South Carolina. On the same runoff night, Tim Scott, a fellow member of the state house, beat South Carolina icon Strom Thurmond's son for the chance to become South Carolina's first black Republican congressman in over a century. I was so happy for my state. I had always known we were better than how we were portrayed in the mainstream media—and better than how some South Carolinians, like Jake Knotts, portrayed us. That night we showed our true face to the country. We weren't just putting an image of backwardness and bigotry behind us. We were at the forefront of a national movement to return government to the people.

Tim Scott's and my victories generated a lot of national attention. The stories were all about how South Carolina was changing and how the Republican Party was changing, and those are good things. But I was grateful that the attention allowed me to talk about the Movement. As I've said, I've always gotten attention because I'm a woman or an Indian American in politics, and I've always felt the need to use that attention to push something bigger.

Around the time of the primary and the runoff, the *New York Times* and the *Washington Post* profiled me. *Newsweek* put me on the cover with the headline "The Face of the New South." They all talked about the usual ugly stuff, the pageant back in Bamberg and the "raghead" remark. But they also gave me a chance to talk about how South Carolinians were demanding votes on the record, reembracing conservative principles, and challenging Washington bailouts. This was the real face of the new South—the face of a people no longer willing to sit back and let others control their destinies. The national media had always looked backward when covering South Carolina. Now they were looking forward for a change. I was thrilled to be their excuse for doing so.

The early general-election polls showed me with a double-digit lead over state senator Sheheen. I faced the challenge, for the first time, of being the front-runner. It was South Carolina, after all, a red state. The press and the pundits expected me to win. All of a sudden, the Republican establishment that I had been critical of was expected to unite behind me to win. Much of that establishment did support me. They knew that even a rock-the-boat reformer like me would pursue the principles they held a lot better than a liberal like my opponent would. But some small segments of the GOP establishment refused to come my way. These were not conservatives in any meaningful way. These were folks who saw government as a way to further their own business interests or in some cases to further a personal political agenda, and I represented a threat to their plans. That was okay with me. I was happy to have the doubters. They only reinforced my natural tendency to campaign like I was the underdog.

From the start, Senator Sheheen had the backing of some well-heeled Republican businessmen who still nursed grudges against Governor Sanford. The board of directors of the South Carolina Chamber of Commerce, after backing Barrett against me in the Republican primary and Sheheen over his competition in the Democratic primary, decided to endorse Sheheen, a trial lawyer, in the general election. To make sure no one missed their point, they made the call before Barrett lost the runoff. The chamber's CEO said it all when he criticized my campaign pledge to hold legislators accountable for their votes.

"I just don't think that's going to be the type of cooperation that we need," he told the Associated Press. "That's a slippery slope when you're talking about getting things done."

The chamber CEO wanted to preserve the kind of "cooperation" that had led to billion-dollar increases in the South Carolina budget each year. But I knew the chamber's decision was the action of its board and didn't reflect the view of most of its members. So I made it

my first order of business in the general election to sit down with busi-
nesspeople who were not political activists. I understood that many of
them had legitimate concerns about the rocky relationship Governor
Sanford had had with the legislature. They didn't want to see a repeat
of that, and I didn't blame them. I explained that, while Governor
Sanford and I shared probusiness principles, I would have a different
approach to working with the legislature. I had served in the house, I
reminded them, and I knew what it took to make the relationship
work. More than that, making South Carolina a business-friendly
state—both to help the businesses we already had and to attract new
ones to our state—was the reason I got involved in politics. I pledged
to reach out to the members of the legislature—not to always agree
with them—but to treat them with courtesy and respect. But I wasn't
about to back down from my bottom line: As governor, my job was to
work for the people of South Carolina, not the legislature.

We made the first major policy proposal of the general election
campaign in a plan to encourage economic growth by, among other
things, eliminating the corporate income tax. Then we launched a
"Less Talk, More Jobs" tour to tell the state about it. Members of the
state house and senate joined me in touring the state talking about
bringing to government the same approach the private sector takes
when it has a problem: not just talking about it but fixing it. That's the
approach we needed for South Carolina jobs. We needed to act on
comprehensive tax reform. We needed to act on changing our workers'
comp system, enacting tort reform, and strengthening our technical
schools so we could match open jobs with qualified workers.

Our message was relentlessly positive and action oriented. I un-
veiled an education-reform package that promised to make South Carolina's more than $11,000-per-child investment in public education
produce a system that worked. We needed to change our funding formula to allow state dollars to follow the child, not fund the bureau-

cracy. And we needed performance-based teacher pay to reward excellent teachers and incentivize other ones. I also introduced a government accountability plan that came out strong for term limits and for reducing the number of statewide elected officials.

While I ran an issues-oriented campaign, my opponent went the other way. Senator Sheheen brought all the skills he had honed as a trial lawyer suing deep-pocketed defendants to his campaign. His strategy from the outset wasn't to offer the voters a choice between two different policy directions for the state but to simply attack me. Later his campaign manager admitted in a forum with Tim that their strategy was lifted straight from the courtroom: to create "reasonable doubt" about what kind of governor I would be. While we talked about jobs and education, Senator Sheheen constantly hammered themes of character and trust. He and his advisers evidently made the decision that they couldn't beat me on the issues, so they devised a campaign based on character assassination and guilt by association.

During the runoff, Congressman Barrett had tried to chip away at my lead by claiming I had failed to disclose some consulting fees for work I did in 2008. I hadn't done anything wrong. I had followed the law, and the South Carolina State Ethics Commission backed me up. But the Barrett campaign seized on the issue as an example of hypocrisy because I had called for income disclosure for legislators. He spent the last days of the runoff pounding me in an attempt to look like a champion of government transparency. It was a strategy that one commentator called trying "to be more Nikki Haley than Nikki Haley."

Barrett's charge was a nuisance issue that we as a campaign hadn't done enough to push back against during the runoff. Sheheen resurrected it in the general election. He also tried to make an issue of my work for the Lexington County Medical Center Foundation, a charity that benefited the Lexington County hospital. He dug into Michael's and my tax returns and tried to spin into a character flaw the fact that we had used extensions and occasionally—like so many Americans—paid fines for late filings. He even went after my parents and our family business. It was all aimed at trying to make himself look more open and transparent than me—to be more Nikki Haley than Nikki Haley.

The second part of his character-assassination campaign strategy was to try to join me at the hip with Governor Sanford. The day after the runoff, Sheheen called me "more of the same." He constantly described my candidacy as offering "four more years of Sanford" and referred to me in the same breath as "those folks who have been running the state for the past eight years." This was his campaign's way of keeping alive the Sanford scandal, and of not so subtly reminding South Carolina of the ugly, unproven allegations of the last two weeks of the Republican primary. Sheheen couldn't very well directly refer to the mud thrown my way, so he used code words and comparisons with Governor Sanford. He talked about having "a governor we can trust" and who "won't embarrass the state." In one of his own ads he put me and Governor Sanford on a split screen with the words "Can we afford another governor who says one thing and does another?" It was another example of the ugly side of South Carolina politics, only this time it was arguably worse. South Carolina voters had already proven what they thought of this kind of politics by giving me a more than two-to-one margin of victory on primary night. Because Sheheen's campaign knew they couldn't directly refer to the discredited allegations, they were playing dirty politics by proxy. At least my earlier accusers had had the courage to own their smear tactics.

This was the substance—or rather, the lack of substance—of my opponent's campaign. He began running television commercials the Thursday after Labor Day. He ran three or four days of positive ads and then began a barrage of negative attack ads that didn't stop until election day. His ads were designed to create fear of me as an unknown—fear of me as someone different in South Carolina politics. While I was crisscrossing the state talking about jobs and education, he was running an ad that featured a series of seemingly everyday South Carolinians rehashing his charges against me and ending with one woman saying, "It makes me think that Nikki Haley isn't who she says she is."

After a Rasmussen poll came out in late September showing my lead growing to seventeen points, a group of disgruntled Republicans decided to go where Sheheen didn't have the political guts to go by directly referring to the unfounded charges in the primary. They called themselves "Conservatives for Truth in Politics," but they were really just members of the old guard who were angry that I had won the nomination and were determined to do anything they could to stop me from winning the governorship. For a while they were headquartered in the offices of the Bauer campaign consultant who had made the second unproven charge against me. They were supported by, among others, none other than that champion of old-style politics at its worst, John Rainey.

We calculated that Senator Sheheen used at least 80 percent of his advertising budget for negative ads. And as the campaign wore on, they began to have an effect. At the beginning of October, polls showed the race narrowing, and Sheheen doubled down on his strategy, releasing his most negative ad of the campaign so far. In mid-October, three weeks before the election, a Winthrop University poll showed the race spread in single digits. My lead had been cut to nine points, forty-six to thirty-seven, with 13 percent of voters still undecided. The disgruntled Republican group held a press conference a few days after the poll came out, resurrecting the five-month-old scandal of the primary. They even ran ads in the last weeks of the campaign. We refused to take the bait. "You know you're within a month of the election when these bogus claims crawl back out of the gutter," our spokesman Rob Godfrey told the press.

The last three weeks of the campaign featured a series of knock-down, drag-out debates. Unfortunately, there were a lot of fireworks but very little fire. While I tried to focus on the issues and get Senator Sheheen to explain his opposition to getting tough on illegal immigration and his support for the Obama health-care plan, he continued his barrage of personal attacks. Every question that he got, it seemed, he managed to bring back around to questioning my character by linking me to Sanford. He would take a question from a recent college graduate about how to improve the job climate for young people in South Carolina and make his answer about how he wanted to put an end to South Carolina "being the butt of late-night TV jokes." As I said, he was a trial lawyer, and he knew how to spin.

The last debate was the worst. It was in Florence, just six days before the election. Here again, even when the questions focused on policy, Sheheen made sure his answers were personal digs at me. I had joined with Tim Scott to fight the billion-dollar mandate that President Obama's health-care plan would impose on South Carolina. I had pledged, as governor, to lead a coalition of governors to fight Obamacare and allow the states to offer real solutions to our health-care crisis. I was dead set against Obamacare, but Sheheen wanted to have it both ways. Pressed on the issue in the debate, he claimed to support some parts of the Obama plan but not others. There were "good and bad" parts of the bill, he insisted.

"Senator, you can't split the cow," I replied. "You can't say you like certain parts of it and not other parts. We're stuck with the whole cow."

Sheheen's answer was petty and insulting, even for him.

"We need a governor with the intelligence and the ability to say when things are good and things are bad," he said.

He was calling me unintelligent! The crowd got it and booed the cheap shot. By the end of the debate, I had had enough. After we had made our closing statements, the moderator asked, as an aside, "Do you two like each other?" He said, "Yes." I said, "I used to."

The general election campaign was frustrating to me for its focus on character assassination when South Carolina had real challenges to confront. I had set out in the campaign to advance a movement, something bigger than any one candidate and any one election. And even after all the negativity, I still believed that there were big, consequential issues at stake. I still believed that the voters, given the choice between being manipulated by scandal and being treated like adults, would choose to take charge of their own destinies. Toward the end, we made an ad that came closer to expressing what I felt was at stake in the election than any other in the campaign. It was just me, wearing a blue turtleneck, talking straight into the camera.

> I've seen how Columbia works. There are two roads you can take. There's the status quo with big spending, special-interest deals, and no reform. Or there's real fiscal discipline, smaller government, and accountability. When you take the conservative road, as I have, you make a lot of insiders mad and they throw a lot of garbage in your way. But that's the road our state needs to take, and that's what I'll do as your governor.

Two roads . . . two choices. I went into election night unsure of whether the voters had gotten a clear picture of the choice before them. The last public poll, taken two weeks before the election, had showed me holding steady with a nine-point lead. At times during the final two weeks, our private polling showed it closer.

We had spent so much time on defense, so much time arguing about things that didn't matter. We had to admit that, while Sheheen had told voters precisely zero about what he would do as governor, he had done a good enough job of mudslinging to create "reasonable doubt" about me in the minds of the electorate.

Michael, the kids, and I spent the first part of election night at the Sheraton Hotel. Meanwhile, our supporters started gathering at the Columbia Convention Center soon after the polls closed at 7:00 P.M. My plan was to stay at the Sheraton until the race was called and then, win or lose, speak to the crowd at the convention center. It was a long and stomach-churning night. When the first returns started coming in around 8:00 P.M., they showed Sheheen in the lead. But it was early, I told myself. Then, a little after eight, the spread flipped and I took the lead. At nine, the lead changed again, with Sheheen taking a narrow margin. And then, later, it was a virtual tie.

There was good news on the national front. The networks were projecting that the Republicans would take back the house. In South Carolina, Tim Scott had made history. The Tea Party was working its magic. But as these positive returns rolled in, my race remained too close to call. Sheheen and I stayed virtually tied for the hour between around 9:00 and 10:00 P.M.

It was one of the longest hours of my life. As I sat there with Nalin on my lap, not sure of what my future would be, my mind traveled to a strange place. There was a wall in the office Tim and I shared in my seventies-style campaign headquarters. We'd started pinning up newspaper clips and other mementos of the campaign on it when we launched in the summer of 2009. By the end of the campaign, it was completely covered with pictures, clips, jokes, cartoons, and other silly stuff. I thought about that wall as I sat there on election night. It was impossible to look at it and not be overcome with gratitude for all the sacrifice it represented. It was all there—my dream team, Jenny, Mitt, Sarah, Henry, and more South Carolinians than I could count. And they were there too: Michael. Rena. Nalin. They had all done so much for me. They had all sacrificed so much. And for what? It couldn't be just to see *me* make history tonight. No. They had given so much so that *South Carolina* would make history come January. As I watched the returns that night, I made a promise to myself—one that I would repeat for everyone to hear later that night. If the voters of South Carolina took a chance on me and elected me their governor, I would never stop working to make them proud.

Just before ten thirty, I started to pull away from Senator Sheheen and build a small lead. The first counties that had come in were the Democratic ones. But as the more conservative counties, like Spartanburg, Greenville, and Horry, came in, my lead grew. Then Lexington County—my home county—came in and pushed me over the edge. It was so cool. The county that had first taken a chance on me in my state house race in 2004 put me over the top in the governor's race in 2010. At 10:40 P.M., the AP called the race. I had won.

Still at the Sheraton, I watched on the television as my supporters cheered at the convention center. Reporters said that history had been made in South Carolina. I was the first female governor. The first minority. The youngest. But none of it seemed real yet. It was just words on a screen.

Then, as if out of nowhere, the South Carolina Law Enforcement Division agents appeared. My security detail. They surrounded me and Michael and the kids. They stayed with us everywhere, scanning the crowd and watching when people got close. Nalin asked, "When are they going to leave?" I said, "They're not going to leave."

And then it was real. I was going to be the next governor of South Carolina.

Chapter Twelve
Transition

In the end, being an underdog was the best thing that could have happened to me. I hadn't had the support of the establishment and old-guard money people in the campaign, so I came into the governor's office not owing anyone. When it came time to make my appointments, I didn't have to return any favors or pay off any debts. I could hire the best and the brightest, and that's what I intended to do.

It was a good thing too. I had a tremendous challenge in front of me. I had promised to return government to the people of South Carolina. That meant wholesale reform of a system that was still very much stuck in the 1800s. The structure of South Carolina's government had been created during Reconstruction following the Civil War. Back then, the (needless to say, white) powers that be had weakened the governorship out of fear that a black man might be elected governor. The result was a system of waste, duplication, and lack of accountability that has survived to this day.

We were up until the wee hours on election night, celebrating and talking to the media. But there was no time to rest on our victory. The very next day, bright and early, Team Haley was back at work. It was difficult at first, making the transition from campaign mode to governing (or pregoverning) mode. We had to give up our 1970s-style headquarters for a windowless, claustrophobic transition office at the capitol. I missed being able to be outside at our old office (even if it was in the parking lot of a strip mall) and feeling the sunshine. Tim missed being able to wear jeans and have a beer at 5:00 P.M. We both survived.

I didn't want to lose the energy and the commitment of the campaign. We had seventy-one days to assemble my executive staff, fill thirteen cabinet agencies, write an inauguration speech, and write a State of the State speech for two weeks later. I knew the worst thing I could do was to get bureaucratic about my staff, bringing on too many people and shackling everybody with job descriptions and rigid zones of responsibility. The secret to our campaign had been that everyone came together and did what needed to be done. Nobody worried about whose job it was to do what. What did Ronald Reagan used to say? "There is no limit to what a man can do or where he can go if he doesn't mind who gets the credit." That was the spirit of our campaign, and it was the spirit I was determined to bring to the governor's office. So I did what any smart businesswoman does: I kept my staff small. I worked my people hard. And I took care of them.

On November 8, just six days after the election, I announced my transition team—the men and women who would help me in making my appointments. The fourteen-member team brought together members of the establishment with members of the reform movement. It was cochaired by former South Carolina house speaker and former U.S. ambassador David Wilkins. He had been speaker when I entered the house in 2004 and had served under no fewer than five governors before going on to be George W. Bush's ambassador to Canada. And that's exactly why I chose him. I didn't want to reinvent the wheel with my transition team. I wanted to learn from the mistakes of others and build on the successes of others. David Wilkins had seen five other governors go through what I was going through. He was the man I wanted to guide my transition to being governor. His cochair, Chad Walldorf, was a Charleston businessman who was a movement conservative and president of the South Carolina Club for Growth who had supported us through the entire campaign.

The job of the transition team was to give me three or four candidates for each cabinet post; then I would make the final call. I don't mind saying that I made the team's job more difficult than it might have been otherwise. I was looking for more than managers, more than caretaker agency heads. I wanted men and women who were dedicated to reforming our state government at a whole new level.

We put a great deal of thought and care into each appointment. I knew that every decision I made mattered. And I was determined to keep the promise I had made on election night to prove to the people of South Carolina that they had made a good decision by electing me governor. But I didn't just want to reinforce the decisions of my supporters. I wanted to change the minds of the people who didn't support me. I wanted them to know that I was going to be a governor for all the people, regardless of whom they voted for. I remember feeling a lot of weight and a lot of pressure with every appointment we announced.

Because I wasn't limited by any need for political payback and wanted to find the very best people, I told my transition team to search nationwide for candidates. I was looking for the best, and interestingly, my first cabinet choice turned out to be right under my nose. Judge William Byars is a tremendously well-respected former family court judge who was Governor Sanford's head of the Department of Juvenile Justice. The department had been under a federal restraining order for thirteen years because of sexual violence and other problems. In less than eight months on the job for Governor Sanford, Byars had the restraining order lifted by transforming the department.

Judge Byars was the man I wanted to lead the Department of Corrections. But Tim, Chad, and supporters in the legislature argued that it was a mistake to take him away from the Department of Juvenile Justice. He had accomplished so much there, they argued, that he was too valuable to move somewhere else. I had a different take on it. My feeling was that people—particularly talented and committed people like Judge Byars—respond to being challenged. And I needed him in the Department of Corrections. Governor Sanford was proud of the fact that, under his previous director, South Carolina had trimmed its corrections budget to the point where it was costing us less to feed inmates than it was costing any other system in the country. That was a good thing, but I wanted more from my prison director. I wanted someone who understood what it means to rehabilitate offenders. What good is it if you're serving the cheapest meal when you're still serving too many of them?

In one sense Judge Byars seemed like an unusual choice for the Department of Corrections. He was known for his love of children. He wore neckties with kids on them. Everyone thought that was the secret to his success at the Department of Juvenile Justice, but I had a feeling there might be more to it. I remember meeting with Judge Byars and his wife, Camille, after I had asked him to be my corrections chief. I asked Camille, "Is that what makes him great—the kids?"

"No," she answered. "It's the challenge."

Judge Byars hadn't made up his mind. He was still considering the offer. But I knew then that I was on the right track. He accepted the appointment (we had to call him on the day of the press conference announcing his nomination and ask him not to wear a tie with kids on it—it wasn't the right look for the Department of Corrections), and his performance has been everything I knew it would be. Judge Byars's appointment was an important one for me, not just because I got the right person for the job but because it gave me new confidence in my decision making. So many people had said that I was wrong to do it, but my gut had told me it was the right move. I knew that if I gave this remarkable man a new challenge, he would rise up to meet it. He hasn't disappointed me.

I knew from the outset that one of my most important picks would be for the Department of Commerce. I needed someone who could bring jobs to South Carolina.

Of four finalists identified by my transition team, I picked Bobby Hitt, a former newspaper editor and now an executive at BMW. I told the press that I liked Bobby because "he knew what it was like on the other side of the red tape." Bobby had represented BMW since the German carmaker had picked South Carolina to build its first full manufacturing facility outside Germany in 1994. That decision had led to over ninety thousand automobile manufacturing jobs in South Carolina and forty new businesses in our state. Bobby had, in fact, been on the other side of the red tape. He knew what businesses were looking for when they made the decision to locate in a state. He knew the process, and he knew how to close a deal. Not only could he recruit new businesses to South Carolina, but he could help me create the environment to make them want to come to our state to begin with.

Bobby's appointment came as something of a surprise to a lot of people. He was the right man for the job, not the right man for the politics. When the *Spartanburg Herald-Journal* published a cartoon of Bobby coming out of a Christmas stocking with the caption "Nikki's Christmas present to South Carolina," I knew I had a, well, . . . a *hit*. As for Bobby, I knew he was going to be great in the job when he showed a businessman's take on the skewed priorities of government. After he was named commerce director, he said one of the hardest parts of his new job was that he now had to carry two phones: one for his son in college for when he called and asked for money and another for everybody else when they called and asked for money.

Under Attorney General McMaster, South Carolina had been one of the original fourteen states that filed suit against Obamacare, challenging the constitutionality of the law. I had supported Henry in that lawsuit, and I was determined that South Carolina not be a victim of the new federal mandate. But I didn't want to stop there. I wanted a director of the Department of Health and Human Services who would work to find solutions to our health-care problem. I wanted someone who wouldn't just say no to the federal plan but who could help me develop solutions of our own—solutions that could then be adopted by other states as alternatives to the Obama plan. I found that man in Louisiana, working for my friend Governor Bobby Jindal.

His name is Tony Keck. He was the first cabinet member I appointed from outside South Carolina. Tony appealed to me because I knew he understood that the point of reforming health care was improving people's lives by improving health outcomes. He understood that one of the main reasons for our out-of-control health-care costs is that we have completely divorced ourselves from the actual cost of health care. People don't see what they're spending, so we're buying a lot of health care we don't really need.

I also went outside South Carolina—all the way to Hawaii—to find my director of the Department of Social Services. Lillian Koller had led a welfare–to-work program under Governor Linda Lingle in which more than 80 percent of the people who went through the program successfully didn't return to welfare. She also reduced the number of children in foster care in Hawaii by half. Again, Lillian was someone who was taking government to the next level—not only making it smaller and more efficient but making it better.

By the time I was finished, I had assembled a team that I knew would make South Carolina proud, and it has. I recently got a call from a Wisconsin legislator who said, "I love what you're doing in South Carolina. How do we do the same?" My answer was simple: We have a great team that is on the job for the right reasons.

About the time the Christmas stocking cartoon appeared in the newspaper, I allowed myself to think I might be winning over the skeptics. I should have known better.

No sooner had I finished naming my cabinet than some members of the Legislative Black Caucus complained of a lack of diversity in my administration. The identity-politics bean counters had done the math. I had appointed nine white men, three white women, and one African American woman. One black caucus member scolded, "There's no excuse in 2011 not to have diversity in the governor's office." I guess the governor herself doesn't count!

The day I made my last cabinet appointment in late January, I met with members of the Legislative Black Caucus to hear their concerns. It was standing room only in my office, and the mood was tense. The legislators made it clear they weren't just angry about my cabinet appointments. I had recently replaced the receptionist in the governor's office, who was a minority, with my longtime and trusted aide, Eileen Fogle, who is white. I listened as the legislators lectured me about how I was obligated to have a cabinet that "looked like South Carolina" and how even my executive staff wasn't the proper color for their tastes. After our closed-door meeting, the legislators had a press conference. One of the members told the media, "I went back [into the governor's office today] and all I did was shake white people's hands. That's offensive."

He was offended? I was offended! In the meeting, I gave the cranky legislators as good as I got. I didn't think about race or gender when I read résumés or made my appointments, I told them. I thought about their qualifications. Period. To me, appointing someone because of their race or gender was the same as appointing them as political payback. In both cases, you were putting politics ahead of performance. At the end of the day, I had to show results as governor. I didn't care what color the people were who helped me do that.

One legislator said to me, "When I go to church, I see a picture of Jesus, a picture of Martin Luther King, Jr., a picture of Barack Obama, and a picture of you. Do you know how bad it hurts that you've done this? What do I tell the people in my church?"

Then I really got angry. To come into my office and tell me that I wasn't sensitive to race was something I couldn't take. "You can't grow up the way I did and come at me like that," I said. "We were the only Indian family in Bamberg. You can't tell me I don't know what you're feeling." I had grown up with a white population that didn't think we were white enough and a black community that didn't see us as minority enough. We were always the "other." My family had suffered too.

I cared about diversity. I cared about having women's voices in my administration. So I told the angry legislators to bring me names. Bring me qualified minority and female candidates for positions in my administration, I said. I promised I would seriously consider them, and if I had the opportunity to hire them I absolutely would. But don't come in here and call me racist, I said. (I never did receive any names from the legislators. But later I appointed Major General Abe Turner to be my director of the Department of Employment and Workforce. He happens to be black—but he also happens to be a retired two-star general and the right man for the job.)

I understood that being elected governor of South Carolina as a female and a minority meant something. But I had never asked to be elected because I was a woman or because I was Indian. For one thing, for those who cared about such things, my race and my sex were at least as much a negative as they were a positive. And for another, when you do that, you're playing the game. You're making promises to special-interest groups—women and minorities—that you are expected to fulfill as governor. I saw my job as governor of all South Carolinians, not of any specific groups.

During the general-election campaign, a group of South Carolina women came to me with a pledge they asked me to sign. It committed me to appointing women to high-level positions in my administration if I were elected governor. My white male opponent immediately signed it. I didn't. I told the group that I wouldn't sign a quota pledge, but I would promise to appoint the best people for the job, regardless of sex. No one is a bigger booster of women in public service than me. But I didn't want to appoint a woman because she was a woman—and I certainly didn't want a member of my team who thought she had a right to be there because she was a woman. I got some heat for this stand. Vince Sheheen used it against me. A "Women for Sheheen" group quickly materialized—to actively oppose the first viable female candidate for governor in South Carolina's history! They even had T-shirts made up. We used to run into them in random places across the state. It was amazing. It was then that I realized these groups—the groups claiming to represent women and minorities—are just like any other establishment special-interest groups. They're looking for politicians who will work for them, not for the taxpayers. But I hadn't spent seven years fighting the old establishment to be bought and paid for by a new establishment.

South Carolina has a shameful history of racial discrimination. Jake Knotts's "raghead" comment during the primary was an ugly reminder that not all of our racism is in the past. Less well publicized was a comment made by an African American member of the South Carolina legislature, Gilda Cobb-Hunter. In an article in the *Atlantic* magazine published after I had won the nomination, Representative Cobb-Hunter called me a "conservative woman with a tan." Unbelievable. The politics of race are ugly, no matter who practices them. Not only that, but racial politics are holding the future of South Carolina— including that of our most vulnerable residents—hostage to old-style, interest-group politics. The members of the Legislative Black Caucus continue to play the race card when it comes to appointments on boards or commissions. They seem to want to keep our state paralyzed by racial consciousness. (They complained when I played my favorite song, "I Gotta Feeling" by the Black Eyed Peas—a mixed-race group they evidently consider a "black" group—when I signed a bill they didn't like that required voters to present identification at the polls. The bill was a victory for the integrity of our elections. I play that song whenever I celebrate!) But South Carolina has had enough of thinking about and judging people on the basis of race. Moving forward means moving beyond that kind of politics, no matter who's playing it.

I think back again to that fruit stand at the side of the road in Lexington County. South Carolina has come so far. The people get that. It's a shame not all of our leaders do.

While Team Haley was tackling the transition, the Haley family was making a transition of its own. During the campaign, Jenny Sanford had talked candidly to Michael and me about family life and the governorship. Her advice reinforced what we already believed about mixing family and politics: Family is number one. Don't let what happened to us happen to you, she said. Protect your family. Protect your marriage.

When I first decided to run for office, I was constantly asked the same question, "Who will take care of your kids?" I will never forget a former Democratic official—a woman—who told me before I ran for the house, "You can't run for office with small kids." As my parents and Michael will tell you, don't say I "can't" do something.

Initially I thought campaigning would be fun for the kids. So I brought them along to one of the first parades I did as a candidate. I was so focused on the volunteers on the float and the balloons and the bumper stickers we were passing out—I never thought about the kids not loving it. What child wouldn't want to ride on a float? But halfway through the parade I looked down from waving to the crowd and saw the kids, then ages two and five. Rena had her arms crossed with a big scowl on her face and Nalin sat there picking his nose. I was mortified! "What's wrong with you guys," I said. "You should be waving!" I got cranky looks back—looks that showed absolutely no willingness to find the fun in riding on a float. So I went into mom mode and said, "You will smile and you will like this!"

Needless to say, they didn't. That night, Michael and I sat the kids down. I said I was sorry about the day. They hadn't asked me to run for office; I shouldn't expect them to smile on command. The Haley family reached a truce that night. I would start asking the kids what they wanted to do, and they would never be made to do anything they didn't want to.

Rena and Nalin became my biggest cheerleaders. During the state house race they would cheer every time we passed one of my campaign signs—"Yay, Mommy!" During the governor's race they would pause the commercials and make us all sit on the couch together to watch them. They watched all the debates from home—they actually wanted to!—and Rena would text me with the online poll results afterward. Rena got so involved she even "interviewed" with Tim for a campaign job during the Republican gubernatorial primary. Here's how she answered some of the "preinterview" questions put to her by Tim:

Why Nikki Haley? "Nikki Haley is my mom and I will support her throughout this campaign."

What in your life experience do you think best qualifies you to be a member of the Haley for Governor team? "Girl

Scouts and tutoring are life experiences that best qualify me for this job because they both involve helping others and being responsible."

What is your greatest strength? "My greatest strength is integrity. I try to always live my life with integrity."

What is your biggest weakness? "My biggest weakness is that I lose focus when I get bored which I am working on."

She was twelve. Look out America!

When it came time for us to move into the mansion, Jenny was wonderful, as usual. She had us over ahead of time and gave us a tour. She helped make the kids feel at home by having Rena and Nalin play the "How many cameras can you find?" game on the mansion grounds. We moved in on inauguration day. Rena and Nalin were completely unfazed by moving into the 156-year-old house. They only had two conditions. First, Rena wanted to make sure that our dog, Simba, was welcome in the house (he was and is). And second, Nalin wanted to have his basketball hoop outside (it's there today, off to the side of the horseshoe driveway in front of the mansion).

As the first family of South Carolina, our lives have settled into what I call our "new normal." On the surface, some significant things changed. But the fundamentals stayed the same.

When you are a candidate, one of the first things you do is make sure you have the support of your family. I have always had the support of Michael in everything I've ever done. What's more, neither my mom and dad nor Michael's parents have ever questioned our choice of public service. They have always been wonderful sounding boards and sources of strength in times of struggle. They have laughed with us, cried with us, and celebrated with us. We are so very blessed to have parents who understand that the life we have chosen is one we want to make a difference with. Whether it is Michael's service in the military or my service in elected office, we have raised our family to know that we are a family of service.

It hasn't always been easy. My brothers and sister have been hassled by the press on more than one occasion. They've been asked for favors to help people they barely know. My family has also had their business hurt because of political opponents trying to get at me. My parents built up a thirty-plus-year business from scratch only to have false things said about them. Regardless of whether it comes with the territory, it's unfair, and Michael and I continue to feel bad about what they've been through.

We've worked hard throughout all of this to keep life as normal as possible for Rena and Nalin. I still see them off to school each morning, and we try to eat dinner together as a family most nights. They go to the same public schools they attended before I was governor. Due to all the normal security concerns that come with being the first family, it's easier to have their friends come over than for them to go out, but we have managed that. Going to birthday parties is a little trickier because it means the kids have to take an additional security guest. But we still have Haley Family Fun Nights every weekend where we play games, watch movies, and eat pizza. And I'm still the undefeated champion of Wii in the Haley house.

They're still just normal kids doing normal kid things. Because the rooms on the first floor of the mansion are used frequently for official business, I told the kids when we moved in that they had to play upstairs. That was the rule. One evening not long after I had become governor, I was hosting a group of senators at the mansion. One of the senior senators walked around the corner into the hallway, and there was a red pigtailed wig on the bust of Governor Ibra Blackwood (1931–35). When I checked around the house, there were colored wigs on all the busts. The kids were playing a joke on the staff. I'm not sure how much the senator appreciated the humor.

As for Michael and me, we try to be the same parents that we've always been; we're just living in a new house now. We spend lots of time checking on the kids and asking plenty of questions so that they know we're there for them. They still come to our room every night. They still love to climb on our bed and talk about things that happened during the day. I hope that never ends. They're at that wonderful age where they're young enough to know that hugs and kisses matter but old enough to understand when something's bothering them and to tell us about it. They can be protective of their time with us. When I'm in public with Nalin, he always asks me to keep my head down so no one will recognize me. He doesn't want any constituents interfering with his time with Mom.

Still, I worry. Life can be hard for a child raised in the public spotlight. That's one of the reasons I've continued the practice, begun during the ugliest part of the campaign, of not watching the news or reading the paper at home. I don't want the kids exposed to the rough-and-tumble of politics. I get clips from my press office and am briefed on stories that matter. With the kids we try to do the same thing. If there is something we feel that people will ask them about, we talk it through with them first.

Throughout it all, they've remained amazingly innocent. Rena came up to me a few weeks back and said, "Are you okay today?" and I said, "I'm okay every day. Why?"

"Nalin and I were watching a show, and the news came on, and it seems like there were some people being mean to you," she said.

I sat both of them down and explained to them that sometimes this can all be one big game. I told them that I'm trying to get things done for our state, and some people may disagree, and that how they handle that disagreement is sometimes not kind and sometimes not very respectful. Either way, I said, I want them to know I can handle it—and that coming home to their sweet, smiling faces always makes all the bad stuff go away.

Michael and I continue to love afternoons on the porch in the rocking chairs. That's how we loved to spend our (rare) free time together before I became governor, and it's something we still do on the porch at the mansion. The upside of life in the governor's mansion is that we no longer have to run to the store to pick up a quart of milk or a gallon of ice cream. The downside is that on date nights we're now accompanied by a security detail. I don't drive anymore, although that's probably a good thing because I think I've forgotten how. Still, I miss my drives, both the quiet ones when I did a lot of my deep thinking and the loud ones when I blew off steam by blaring Joan Jett on the radio.

Michael still puts on a uniform every day for his job in the South Carolina Army National Guard. He continues to be away occasionally for training and could be deployed at any time. We are dealing with that possibility like any other military family. We've prepared the kids. We cherish our time together, and we know we will be praying for the day when he comes home safe.

As for the title we use for Michael these days, he's settled on "first gentleman" (but then, he always did like the formal, military approach to titles). I prefer "coolest first man ever," and I say it a lot, which he isn't crazy about. There's never been a first gentleman in South Carolina government before, so we've had to make some adjustments. Instead of having first ladies' teas and things like they've done in the past, we've taken all those kinds of events and made them first family events. We have Easter egg hunts and Christmas celebrations and other things for the whole family. When Michael can't escape going to a tea or something equally girly, I go with him to protect his macho rep.

I've said it before, but I have been truly blessed to have a husband like Michael who supports me unconditionally. Not only that, but he is an amazing and trusted adviser to me. When I'm fighting for something, he is the calm voice at the end of the day that says, "Pull back; you're being too aggressive" or "Fight harder; this is the right thing." He's a wonderful partner and a fantastic dad. I love how he can wrestle on the floor with Nalin or go for a run with Rena. I love how he knows what I need when I need it. I don't know how anyone does this job without having a spouse who is truly there for them, in the good times and bad. They say that political life is only for the strong at heart. You have to have someone who keeps your heart strong. Michael will always be that strength for me.

All in all, it's a pretty good life. It's the life we chose. One of no regrets. One in which I hope that people will know we were here and, in the end, be able to say that South Carolina was better because of us. That's my dream. I work every day to make it a reality.

Chapter Thirteen
The First 250 Days

On the campaign trail I used to say that Rena and Nalin remind me every day that I'm just a mom. At no time was that more true than the night before I was inaugurated as governor of South Carolina.

I had been up into the wee hours taking care of Rena, who was fighting the flu and throwing up all night. I had a full-blown ear infection myself. And to top it off, South Carolina was experiencing truly bizarre weather. Columbia had been hit with a rare snowstorm that had turned into treacherous freezing rain. Because of the dangerous conditions, we had to postpone family fun night at the fairgrounds.

Long story short: On inauguration day I was tired, I was on major antibiotics, and it was cold. There was a prayer service before the swearing in, and I found myself sweating the small stuff and being a mom. Who would make sure my parents made it to the church? Was Rena well enough to be there?

The service was in Trinity Cathedral, across the street from the statehouse. Ministers from different churches across the state came to speak. Governor Sanford was there, as was Jenny and other former governors and members of the general assembly. It was the most beautiful church service I have ever been to. It was so much more than just another event on an eventful inauguration day. The ministers led us all in a prayer for our state and its leaders. One spoke directly to me. "With the help of God, you can change political history," he said. I was so moved and so energized. To me the service couldn't have been more relevant to what was about to happen. As I had always said, I am a woman who understands that through the grace of God all things are possible. That morning I felt that grace like I never had before. As I left the church, it was as if all my sickness left me.

We walked through the snow back across the street to the statehouse. They rushed Michael, the kids, and me into a holding room where my mom and dad, the rest of my family, Tim, Jon, and some of our friends were waiting. When everyone was situated, all the pictures had been taken, and the hugs had been had, the event organizers took me upstairs. The ceremony would be outside, on the south steps of the statehouse. In keeping with tradition, Governor Sanford and I would walk down the steps together to the podium and dignitaries on the platform below, where I would take the oath of office and give my inaugural address.

While Governor Sanford and I were waiting to start the walk down the steps to begin the ceremony, one of the police officers who were lining the steps of the capitol collapsed. The paramedics were called, and the officer was taken to the hospital for observation. The officer turned out to be fine, but the incident delayed the start of the ceremony for about fifteen minutes. (Funny story: After the officer collapsed, someone called out, "Is there a doctor here?" Several Indian American friends and relatives came rushing forward. It really cracked up my brother Mitti. What kind of question was that at the inauguration of an Indian American governor? Of course there was a doctor in the house!)

While the ceremony was delayed, Governor Sanford and I had a while to stand together at the top of the stairs. I looked down and saw what seemed like a sea of people—waiting.

"I'm nervous," I told the governor.

"Don't worry," he said. "You're going to be fine."

"You'll let me know if I mess up?"

"You won't mess up."

And with a final "Are you ready?" from Governor Sanford, we began our walk down the steps. Everything seemed to happen in slow motion. The first thing I saw was the bright burgundy of my father's turban. He and my mother were seated on the platform, along with Michael's parents, next to all the living former governors, constitutional officers, and other dignitaries. Right where they belonged. Michael and the kids were seated next to them. I looked out into the audience and saw my sister and brothers. I saw Tim and Jon sitting together. I saw all of them and I thought, *How did we do this?* I didn't know how I had gotten to this day, but I knew I hadn't gotten there alone.

Taking the oath of office with Michael and the kids in front of our family and friends is one of the most cherished memories I have. The emotion was overwhelming. We had overcome so much. We had so much to accomplish! But being on that platform as the first female governor in South Carolina history in front of my mom, who was unable to become a judge because of the limitations of being a woman in India, was the most rewarding. I hoped that this day wiped away the hurt of the challenges she had faced. I hoped it was a vindication for both my parents, proof that they had made the right choice in choosing to raise their family in a country of unlimited opportunity.

In my inaugural address I thanked all those people who had

helped me. I said it was "a day for new beginnings." And I quoted former British prime minister Margaret Thatcher: "Once we concede that public spending and taxation are [more] than a necessary evil, we have lost sight of the core values of freedom."

It wasn't Mrs. Thatcher's most poetic quote, but I liked it because it expressed so well what I wanted for South Carolina. I wanted the people to be awakened to a new role for their government. I wanted them to understand that their money is theirs—government has no prior claim to it. I wanted them to understand that their freedom is theirs, that it's not the gift of their government but of their creator.

I spoke of a vision for South Carolina that draws its energy and inspiration not from the statehouse that stood behind me but from the people who stood before me. I ended by echoing the words of someone who knew a little bit about government of, by, and for the people, Abraham Lincoln.

"So, with faith in God, who knows what is right, and faith in our own ability to use the skills and judgment He gives us to do what is right, we can make this vision a reality."

On January 19, seven days after I was sworn in, I gave my first State of the State speech before the general assembly. It was an amazing evening. The entire general assembly was gathered in the house chamber. The sergeant at arms announced me, and as I walked down the center aisle shaking hands and hugging members, I watched in awe as the chamber rose to its feet in applause. This was the same place where I had been punished for defying the leadership. The same place where I had been shunned as a troublemaker and an outsider.

I had come a long way from being the freshman who couldn't get anyone but Nathan to sit with me during lunch. But our state had a long way to go. I laid out our challenges on jobs, education, health care, prisons, and restructuring our antiquated government. We were faced with an $800 million budget shortfall, the largest in our history. We have a shared responsibility, I said, to move the state forward. I challenged the legislature to change its culture so we wouldn't be talking about the same set of challenges when I met them again in a year.

I had seen the legislative culture firsthand, and I was determined to fix it. "It's slow, it's political, and it doesn't have to be," I said. The key was to remember who we work for. I quoted Abraham Lincoln, who once said, "The people will save their government if the government itself will allow them."

"To the legislators seated before me," I said, "I ask that you let the people save us. Let them in. They have spoken loud and clear."

We had to get our own house in order. That meant, first and foremost, conquering our budget deficit. We needed to be honest about the challenge before us. "This budget year is going to hurt," I said. But from that pain could come the opportunity for us to reprioritize our government, to make it more responsive to the people and more responsible with the taxpayers' money.

Getting our house in order also meant not playing Washington, D.C.'s games anymore. I announced that I had instructed my cabinet to stop chasing federal dollars just to grow their budgets. "The days are over when Washington tells us, 'If you want the money, jump,' and South Carolina responds, 'How high?'" I said.

"Starting tonight, South Carolina is a state that is focused on establishing our own financial independence, controlling our own destiny, and empowering our own people with the knowledge that their state government doesn't jump for anyone."

It felt good. I hadn't stood at that podium since I had made my maiden speech as a newly elected house member six years earlier. So much had changed. But I wasn't kidding myself. I knew we couldn't all just hold hands together and make our differences disappear. I knew there would be battles down the road. But for a night, at least, we put our differences aside for the sake of the state we all loved.

Everyone seemed to sense that a shift had taken place. Forty-five minutes earlier, as I had worked my way up the aisle after entering the chamber, I had come upon an older Democratic legislator with whom I had served on a committee. During the campaign, he had once pulled me aside and warned me that I could never win. "I've watched you for a long time, and you have a promising career," he said. "I know how mean Republican politics in this state can be. They will chew you up and spit you out. You need to get out."

That night, as I had walked by him, the older legislator had reached out his hand and taken mine. "I was wrong," he had said. I had given him a hug and replied, "I'm glad you were. Thank you for trying to look out for me."

My first priority in office was to establish a good working relationship with the legislature. That relationship had frayed during the Sanford years. Too many members of the general assembly hadn't trusted my predecessor, and they expected me to be more of the same. But I was different. I had once been in their shoes. I knew what they wanted and what they needed.

My team and I came to realize pretty quickly that little things can mean a lot—the common courtesies that demonstrate respect, like letting members know when you're coming to their district. One of the first things I did to try to restore some sense of respect was to establish an open-door policy in the governor's office. Members of the legislature could come by anytime to talk. It didn't matter if they were Democratic or Republican, and lots of them took me up on the invitation. Some of the Democrats who came to visit had never been in the governor's office before.

The one thing I wasn't willing to do to keep our legislators happy was play pork-barrel politics. This meant I had to find other ways to build support for my agenda. Mostly this effort just meant my staff and I had to do a lot of good old, time-consuming work. One legislator desperately wanted a Walmart in his district, but the company didn't seem interested at all. So we called Walmart and asked the company to take a look and see if it was interested. It sent out a site unit and talked to the legislator. We didn't spend anybody's money or promise anybody anything. We just put in a little extra effort, and we built a good relationship with that legislator.

Hands down, the biggest surprise I have had as governor is how much the federal government won't let me do my job. From health care to illegal immigration to job-killing regulations, we have a president and a Washington, D.C., crowd that think they know better than we do. Not only that, but they think there's a one-size-fits-all answer to all our problems, as if South Carolina were the same as California or Michigan. I hate to say it, but Washington has been the single biggest obstacle for me to creating jobs and improving the lives of South Carolinians.

One of the first issues I had to fight the feds on was health-care reform. I have been consistent as a candidate and as governor in my opposition to Obamacare. The president's approach is wrongheaded and unconstitutional. He's pouring more costs into the system through federal mandates instead of taking costs out of the system through transparency and individual responsibility.

But there is one bright side to the president's plan: It has sparked a conversation about health care that is badly needed. Our health-care problem is real. In South Carolina, we have a large Medicaid population, and health care is the main driver of our budget deficits. But our health-care problem is also unique to our state—it's not the same as the health-care challenges in states like Massachusetts or Nebraska. Our challenges are mainly poverty and education. We have good services, but we need to educate people on how to better utilize them and on how to pay more attention to their health.

I brought this up with President Obama before I took office. In December 2010 the president had all the governors-elect up to Washington for a meet and greet with his administration. All the different cabinet secretaries came to see us and told us about what they do. Then we had lunch with the president and the vice president. For reasons that are not entirely clear to me, the White House seated me at the table with Vice President Biden, directly in front of where the president was speaking. We had a nice lunch. I had the opportunity to have a long talk with the vice president.

After we ate, President Obama made some remarks and then opened up the discussion to questions from the governors-elect. Scott Walker, the incoming governor of Wisconsin, asked the first question about more flexibility in federal funding to states. Then the president called on me. I told him that his health-care plan imposed mandates that South Carolina just couldn't afford. Our annual budget is five billion dollars, and we had calculated that his plan would cost us five billion dollars over the next ten years. We expected to see 30 percent to 40 percent of our private companies drop their employees' coverage and force their workers into the public system. My question had two parts, I told the president. Would he repeal Obamacare? And if not, would he allow South Carolina to opt out of the system?

It was no surprise that President Obama answered that as long as he was president he wasn't going to allow repeal of his signature legislative accomplishment. On the second part of my question he was a little more conciliatory—a little. He said he would consider letting South Carolina opt out under three conditions. First, that we set up a statewide insurance exchange. Second, that we create a state-subsidized insurance pool. And third, that we cover preexisting conditions.

I appreciated the opportunity to talk to the vice president and president, I really did. But I sat down again feeling like the president's real answer had been "no" to both parts of my question. South Carolina couldn't really opt out of Obamacare. If we managed to put in place a plan that met all his conditions, I thought, we'd end up with the same expensive, inflexible system that was mandated by the federal law.

After the president called on another half dozen or so of my new colleagues, the governors-elect seemed to run out of questions for him. In the uncomfortable silence that came next, I looked at Tim, who was sitting across the table from me. Should I ask another question? He shrugged, and so I did. I asked the president about South Carolina's Savannah River site, a Department of Energy facility that has created thousands of jobs in our state. Nuclear material temporarily stored at the site had been scheduled to be permanently disposed of in Yucca Mountain in Nevada. The taxpayers had already paid $20 billion to develop Yucca Mountain, including $1.2 billion from South Carolina taxpayers. But the previous year, the Obama administration had canceled further work on the project. "Will you keep the promise made to the people of my state and reopen Yucca Mountain?" I asked. The president said no. "Then give us our money back." I said. He told me he would have Secretary of Energy Steve Chu call me. Later the secretary did call. He told me South Carolina couldn't have its money back because the feds needed it. I told him that when I go to Best Buy and pay for something that hasn't come in yet, I get my money back if it doesn't come in. What's the difference here? Let's just say that the secretary was not persuaded by my argument.

The next time I talked to the president about health care was in February, at a National Governors Association (NGA) meeting in Washington. (As an aside, I want to take this opportunity to clarify something. A photo from the NGA meeting with the president showed me typing on my iPad as the president spoke. Let it be known that I was paying attention—I am a constant note taker. I was not playing Angry Birds!)

A few weeks before the NGA meeting, Judge Roger Vinson, a federal judge in Florida, had ruled that the individual mandate in Obamacare is unconstitutional. Because the mandate was inseparable from the rest of the plan, Judge Vinson declared the entire law unconstitutional. It was a tremendous victory for South Carolina and America. This was the challenge that Attorney General McMaster had joined on behalf of South Carolina the previous year. Twenty-six states had charged that Obamacare was unconstitutional, and a federal court had agreed.

Judge Vinson's ruling should be required reading for anyone who cares about states' rights and individual liberty. He argued that a federal government that can mandate that individuals buy something— health insurance, for instance—is a federal government that can mandate anything. America has a Constitution of enumerated powers—it clearly defines what the federal government can do and leaves the rest to the states and the people. "If Congress can penalize a passive individual for failing to engage in commerce," the judge wrote, "the enumeration of powers in the Constitution would have been in vain."

Judge Vinson's ruling was great, but it was not definitive. Other judges had found all or parts of the law to be in accordance with the Constitution. For states struggling to develop budgets and move forward on health care, the need for clarity was more urgent than ever. So the day after the ruling, I went on *Fox & Friends* and announced that I was going to recruit governors to sign a letter to President Obama asking him to expedite a Supreme Court ruling on the law. Judge Vinson's ruling was an important victory. But the final outcome was still uncertain. States like mine that wanted to move forward with their own solutions were stuck in limbo. If the law is as important as the president says it is, I told Brian Kilmeade, he should want to see the Supreme Court rule "yesterday."

My announcement took my staff by surprise (not for the first or the last time). But one of the things I had pledged in the campaign was to lead a coalition of governors to oppose Obamacare and propose our own health-care solutions. This seemed like an obvious place to start. So we scrambled and got to work. By the time we were finished, twenty-nine governors had joined me in signing the letter. At the NGA meeting, I asked the president if he would join the thirty governors who had signed the letter in seeking an expedited ruling one way or the other. He copped out and told me he would neither expedite the high-court ruling nor stall it. But in a welcome surprise two weeks later, he joined us and asked the court to expedite the case.

My wrangling with the president aside, I've always seen it as my duty as governor not to simply fight the mandates in Obamacare. My goal is to go a step further and say, okay, if the Obama plan isn't the way to go, how do we fix the problem? The easy way out is to just say what we're against. The hard thing is to come up with what we're for. I think that's a discussion the states and the governors are best suited to lead. We're a big country, with different economies and cultures in different states. Some ideas are going to work for some states and not others. But that's the point of the system of government that we have. Our republic works best when we follow the Tenth Amendment and honor states' rights.

As for South Carolina's contribution to this discussion, as I've said, I'm an accountant. Numbers tell me if an individual or a business is spending wisely. The problem is that today Americans aren't seeing the numbers we need to make good choices for our health. We're completely divorced from the cost of health care.

I like to use the analogy of getting your car fixed. Before you pay for repairs on your car, you see an estimate of what the bill will be. But when it comes to our health, we have no idea what we're spending. We go to the doctor or hospital, we receive services, but we never see a price tag. We have no idea if we're getting our money's worth. Our insurance or the government pays the bill, and we pay (or the taxpayers pay) ever-higher premiums. It's no wonder that we have so many individuals who can't afford insurance, small businesses that can't afford to insure their employees, and Medicaid and Medicare costs that are busting our budgets.

To move costs out of the system and make informed choices for our health, we need to be able to know the true cost of the health care we consume. That means an open market for health care, with the choices and price information that make a market function. We need to allow insurance companies to cross state lines to encourage competition and give people more choices of plans. And we need to restructure our tax and entitlement systems to create real transparency between patients and doctors and between doctors and insurance companies.

When we do that, I'm certain we will reduce health-care costs by cutting out things we don't need or things we already get somewhere else. We will be better, more informed consumers, and health-care providers will be forced to compete for our business. We will start driving costs out of the system rather than bringing new costs into the system under the president's plan. And more important, we will see patients beginning to get involved in their own health care and care more about their health. That, in the end, is what this conversation should be about—not costs, not programs or bureaucracies, but our health and the quality of life that good health brings.

Another issue I've had to fight Washington tooth and nail on is illegal immigration. Even before I was governor, I knew tackling this issue would be a battle royal. The previous year, I had watched as Governor Jan Brewer of Arizona signed a state law to do what Washington refused to do—tackle the illegal immigration crisis in her state. For her efforts, Brewer was vilified as racist by the president and the media. Not only that, but she was sued by the Obama Justice Department to prevent the law from ever being implemented.

Still, I wasn't prepared for the degree of resistance I received. In South Carolina we already had a strong anti–illegal immigration bill when I became governor. All I wanted to do was enforce it, but the Obama administration managed to stand in the way of my doing even that.

Our law required businesses to prove they weren't hiring illegal aliens by using, among other methods, a federal database called E-Verify. This system is designed to make it easy for businesses to know if they are employing legal residents or not. Employers simply type in the Social Security number provided by the applicant, and the system tells them if the number is legitimate. The problem is, for E-Verify to work government has to know whether employers are actually using it.

Shortly after I became governor, the Department of Homeland Security told us we could no longer audit businesses to see if they were using E-Verify. The privacy of the people being checked, they said, would be compromised if we asked for proof from businesses. That decree put the twenty-four state employees in our Labor, Licensing and Regulation Department at a standstill just as they were starting to make real progress under the law. Out of the more than six thousand businesses they had checked, over two thousand violations had been found. But no more. Now the federal government was saying that we couldn't use the best and most efficient means we had to enforce our law.

My goal wasn't to overburden employers with rules and regulations. I just wanted to use the easiest and least costly way to ensure we weren't employing illegals, and that was E-Verify. So my Labor Department director, Catherine Templeton, started calling the Department of Homeland Security to resolve the situation. Months went by and she received no definitive answer. So I called Homeland Security secretary Janet Napolitano myself. Still—unbelievably—there was no answer. She wouldn't return my phone call. So I held a press conference.

"South Carolina has had to fight this administration on multiple issues," I said. "We are fighting them on health care. We are fighting them on being able to create jobs. It is absolutely ludicrous that we are now fighting the fact that we can't even enforce our own illegal immigration laws."

I promised to keep up the pressure on President Obama's administration until I got an answer. And lo and behold, within a week not only had I heard from the secretary, but we had resolved the issue. We could now enforce our illegal immigration law.

It was a victory of sorts, but I wanted to do more than just fight with Washington to enforce a three-year-old law. South Carolina experienced a 1,000 percent jump in the number of illegal immigrants in our state between 1990 and 2004. The Mexican drug cartels, which increasingly control illegal immigration on the southwestern border, are active in 230 U.S. cities, including at least four in South Carolina. South Carolina sits right between Atlanta and Charlotte, both cities with a growing and dangerous cartel presence. Much like Arizona, we couldn't afford to wait for Washington to do something. So in June 2011 we passed a law that mirrors the Arizona illegal immigration law. It gives our law enforcement officers the ability to question people about their immigration status in the course of enforcing other laws. It was a measure that I had cosponsored in the state house and championed on the campaign trail. I was happy to sign it as governor.

Unsurprisingly, before I had the chance to put pen to paper, the

ACLU announced it would sue to prevent the law from being implemented, just as the Obama administration had done in Arizona. Even though the law explicitly prohibits it, the ACLU claimed that our law would lead to racial profiling. This is an old and tiresome argument. Pro–illegal immigration groups and, quite frankly, the Obama administration constantly want to make illegal immigration a racial issue. They say those who want to crack down on illegal immigration are being insensitive to minorities. They say they're shocked to see me, a minority governor, doing such a thing. They could not be more wrong, about me and about illegal immigration.

I am the proud daughter of legal immigrants—emphasis on the *legal*. My parents played by the rules and waited their turn. They are offended—as am I—by those who try to backdoor the system and come here illegally. When we allow this debate to be about race, we lose sight of the principle that is really at the heart of it: the rule of law. We are a nation of immigrants, and we're proud of it. But we are first and foremost a nation of laws. If we give up being a nation of laws, we give up everything this country was founded on.

Laws like ours in South Carolina and the Arizona law aren't the final answer to our illegal immigration problem, and they're not trying to be. The true solution is for the federal government to do its job and secure the border. But until it does that, the states have a job to do. In South Carolina we're not about to be intimidated by lawsuits and racial name-calling. If pro–illegal immigration groups had a better argument for their policies, they'd be using it. The fact that they've resorted to calling their opponents names says everything about the policy ground they stand on. We take enforcing our laws seriously in South Carolina, even if Washington doesn't.

Fighting Washington on health care and illegal immigration had been bad enough, but in April the unbelievable happened. One Saturday Tim called me at home after being contacted by Mike Luttig, a former federal judge who was now Boeing Corporation's executive vice president and general counsel. The National Labor Relations Board (NLRB)—a six-member panel tasked with enforcing federal labor law—was preparing to sue Boeing for building its 787 Dreamliner assembly plant in South Carolina. The board was alleging that Boeing's decision to locate the production line in South Carolina was an illegal labor practice. Unlike Washington State, where Boeing's other 787 assembly line is located, South Carolina is a right-to-work state where workers can't be forced to join a union. If the NLRB was successful in the lawsuit, it could halt 787 production in our state and all the job creation and business development that went with it.

When Tim told me the news, I first thought he was making a joke—I actually thought he was trying to make me laugh. Everything I was hearing was so completely un-American. Boeing came to North Carolina because the cost of doing business here is low, our state has a loyal and committed workforce, and our infrastructure is strong—in addition to the fact that we are a right-to-work state. Now we have a board of unelected bureaucrats telling a private company where it could locate? Can that happen in America?

When I saw the actual complaint, filed four days later on April 20, I realized that it *could* happen in America. The lawsuit charged that Boeing had illegally retaliated against its largest union, the International Association of Machinists (IAM), when it opened a second assembly line in South Carolina. The machinists had struck four times since 1989 at Boeing's facility in Puget Sound, Washington. Their latest strike, in 2008, had gone on for eight weeks and cost the company $100 million a day. Production of the 787 was two years behind schedule when Boeing made the decision to come to South Carolina. When, I wondered, did it become illegal for a company to want to deliver a product on time?

It's difficult to convey the impact Boeing's 2009 announcement that it was coming to North Charleston had had on South Carolina. It was the answer to a prayer. It was more than just another company deciding to locate in our state. There are only a handful of places in the entire world where large commercial aircraft are fully assembled, and now Charleston was going to be one. And when a state is successful in pulling in an industry leader like this, the benefit includes much more than just the jobs created by the company itself. There is a multiplier effect that transforms a state.

We had seen this effect after BMW located its first manufacturing facility outside Germany in South Carolina in the early 1990s. The company had predicted two thousand employees at its height but now have more than seven thousand and it's not done yet. More than that, though, its presence in South Carolina created tens of thousands of additional jobs and forty new businesses in fields associated with automobile manufacturing. Like BMW, Boeing was a vote of confidence—a billion-dollar vote of confidence—in the business environment and the workers of South Carolina. When the 787 Dreamliners—those "mack-daddy planes," as I call them—start rolling out of the North Charleston plant in 2012, they will be the first aircraft assembled by Boeing outside the Pacific Northwest. We were proud to have inspired such confidence from such a great American company.

So imagine our surprise and shock when the federal government told us it was illegal.

It was a transparently political lawsuit. The NLRB's claim that Boeing was illegally retaliating against its unionized workers was totally, off-the-charts, on-its-face ridiculous. At the same time that Boeing was creating one thousand jobs in Charleston, it had created an additional two thousand jobs at its 787 plant in Washington. Not a single unionized employee was hurt by the company's move to South

Carolina. When I heard this, I wondered how the government could credibly claim that a company has "retaliated" against a union when it has expanded the union's membership by two thousand. It couldn't. The only conceivable motive for the lawsuit was to send a message to companies thinking about locating in right-to-work states like South Carolina. This was President Obama's handpicked union cronies at the NLRB scoring points with their labor base by trying to make the unions relevant. It wasn't going to work.

At a news conference the next day I unleashed. "I will absolutely not allow them to bully our businesses or mess with our employees," I said. "On behalf of all the twenty-one governors of right-to-work states, I would respectfully ask the president to get his bureaucrats off the backs of our businesses." Our two South Carolina senators, Jim DeMint and Lindsey Graham, joined me in the fight, as did other right-to-work state lawmakers like Tennessee senator Lamar Alexander and Kentucky senator Rand Paul. It was amazing to us how the president could miss—much less intend—the message the lawsuit was sending to business. Not only does the NLRB lawsuit discourage companies from locating in right-to-work states, but it discourages them from locating in forced-union states as well. Under the Obama NLRB, if you locate your business in a forced-union state like Washington, you can never expand beyond it because doing so, apparently, is illegal. In the end, all the lawsuit does is encourage jobs to go overseas. If right-to-work states are illegal and unionized states are traps, what's the other option?

In an economy desperate for jobs, this was the absolute last thing the federal government should be doing to an American company. As far as I was concerned, the lawsuit was more than just a South Carolina issue. If a board of unelected union apologists could get away with telling a private company where it could and could not locate its business, there would be no end to the union bullying.

This fight was personal to me in more ways than one. Months before the NLRB lawsuit—when my governorship wasn't a week old—the machinists had sued me for talking smack about the unions in South Carolina. They didn't like it when I touted the union-fighting skills of my new director of labor. "We're going to fight the unions, and I needed a partner to do it," I said at the news conference announcing her appointment. The audacity! Evidently the unions weren't used to that kind of candor. Their spokesman told the press, "This is practically unprecedented for a state to be so clear and so overt." Well, forgive me for being clear and overt, but I am unapologetic in my opposition to forced unionization in South Carolina. Both our employers and our employees understand that direct communication—not union extortion and work stoppages—is the key to jobs and economic growth.

I may have been the first governor to have a board of unelected bureaucrats so brazenly try to punish her state for being antiunion, but I was also determined to be the last. No lawsuit was going to stop me from fighting the unions and fighting the NLRB—and being loud about it. In May I called on GOP presidential candidates debating in South Carolina to let the voters know where they stood on the issue. I met with the U.S. Chamber of Commerce in Washington and demanded that the president also speak up on the lawsuit. Did he agree with the board he had appointed or not? In June I recruited fifteen other governors to sign with me a letter to the NLRB's acting general counsel. I testified before Congress, telling Chairman Darrell Issa and the House Oversight and Government Reform Committee that the lawsuit would not only send American jobs overseas but also make foreign companies think twice about locating in the United States.

While we were fighting to keep the federal government at bay, the Charleston plant had its grand opening on June 10, 2011, six months ahead of schedule. The event attracted a crowd of Boeing officials, plant workers, and exuberant South Carolina politicians. Everyone was excited to see the new facility. It was a brutally hot Palmetto State day, and the organizers had unaccountably set up the ribbon-cutting ceremony out in the blazing sun. The guys from the Pacific Northwest were wilting in the heat. By the time the speechifying and the ribbon cutting were over, even we South Carolina natives were feeling it. Then, just when we thought we couldn't take another second out in the heat, there was music. I heard the familiar sound of the Black Eyed Peas rocking "I Gotta Feeling." As the music cranked up, the gigantic doors of the facility started to open. Cool, air-conditioned air rushed out as we rushed into the 1.1-million-square-foot plant. The facility truly has to be seen to be believed. It is the size of eleven football fields—big enough for the 787s that are produced in it to make a U-turn as they are assembled inside.

Those mack-daddy planes began being assembled at the Charleston plant last summer. The first Dreamliners built in South Carolina will be flying this year. At about the same time production started in Charleston, a U.S. District Court judge there tossed out the machinists' lawsuit against me. He said it was my First Amendment right to talk smack about the unions, which is good, because I have no intention of stopping. And do you know what the best thing is? The more I talk smack, the more I have businesses calling me wanting to come to South Carolina. They see a state that wants their business. They see a governor who will fight for them. As long as I'm leading South Carolina, that's not going to change.

Beyond the lesson that conservative judges matter, the biggest revelation for me in this whole fiasco is how hard I've had to fight to do something that is so common sense. I have no greater priority than creating jobs in South Carolina. It is my mission. I eat, sleep, and breathe bringing new employers to my state. That I would have an administration in Washington actively opposing my creating jobs is something I never dreamed would happen.

In my first nine months as governor, we announced over 15,000 new jobs in South Carolina. I say "announced" because government doesn't create jobs. Government can only create the conditions that allow entrepreneurs to create jobs. South Carolina is a right-to-work state for precisely that purpose—we've seen the job-killing effects of forced-union laws. I support keeping taxes low on individuals and small businesses because when businesses have extra cash they create jobs. I've fought Washington regulations, not out of ideology or politics but because they kill jobs. The Small Business Administration estimates that the total cost to American small businesses of complying with federal regulations was $1.75 trillion in 2008—$1.75 trillion that could have gone to creating jobs. And that doesn't even take into account all the new regulations in Obamacare. If Congress and the president were serious about putting Americans back to work, they would declare a moratorium on new federal regulations immediately.

The government doesn't create jobs. The private sector creates jobs—*Boeing* has created jobs in Washington State and in South Carolina. The only thing government can do is influence the environment in which jobs will either be created or be destroyed. Unbelievably, the Obama administration has chosen to poison the environment for job creation in South Carolina and beyond. I can't say it any more plainly than this: Their action won't be allowed to stand. Not on my watch.

In the time that I have been governor, there hasn't been a day when I haven't thought about that promise I made on election night. The voters of South Carolina took a chance on me, and I work every day to make them proud.

The new spirit of predictability and cooperation I've tried to build with the legislature has paid off in a string of significant accomplishments for the state. In addition to our historic illegal immigration bill, we passed a voter ID law this year. My thinking on this was pretty straightforward. If you need to show your ID to buy Sudafed or get on an airplane, it's a no-brainer that you should show your ID to protect the integrity of our elections. The critics said requiring ID would disenfranchise thousands of voters who would have trouble getting identification. The doomsayers confidently predicted that thousands of people would lose their right to vote because they couldn't get an ID. So I told the people, "If you're having trouble, give me a call; we'll help you out." I even said I would drive them down to the DMV myself— and I meant it! We ended up driving twenty-five people to the DMV, all of whom we helped get their ID.

We enacted tort reform this session as well. South Carolina was the last state in the southeast that didn't have a cap on runaway lawsuit awards, and now we have one. I told people the choice was simple: You're either for business or for the trial lawyers. South Carolina chose businesses. But it's just a start. We have more reform to do next year.

We also reformed Medicaid. We were the only state that didn't negotiate its Medicaid rates with health-care providers. Every year the hospitals and nursing homes would descend on Columbia with their hands out, and we didn't even try to find any bargains. No more. Now my Health and Human Services chief is able to negotiate lower spending on Medicaid. And the remarkable thing is that we now have providers coming to us to point out areas where we can save money.

And—miracle of miracles!—after over three years of struggle, we finally made on-the-record voting permanent law in South Carolina. Now every legislator has to show every single vote on the record. My favorite part of the legislation, however, is that legislators also have to show how they vote on every section of the budget. We can now see exactly who supported what when it comes to our tax dollars. At long last, South Carolinians can go into the next election actually knowing how the men or women they're being asked to return to office have spent their money and steered their state.

Interestingly, several of the legislative leaders I had previously tangled with became good allies in that first session. As a house member, I had not known the senate leaders all that well. Majority Leader Harvey Peeler and Finance Chairman Hugh Leatherman had notoriously clashed with Governor Sanford on fiscal policies. But when I got to know them I found them refreshingly open to trying new things and pursuing a more conservative agenda. Even House Speaker Bobby Harrell, who had opposed me so strongly on requiring votes on the record, was enormously helpful on voter ID, Medicaid reform, tort reform, and other items on our agenda. Politics is funny that way. Old wounds can often be overcome for the good of the state, and I welcomed and appreciated the support of these legislators.

We were tremendously successful legislatively this first year, but we were less successful when it came to the budget. I made it clear to the legislature in the State of the State address that I was going to strictly observe spending caps. We would take what we spent for each part of government last year and adjust it for population and inflation, and that would be it. Anything extra should either pay down debt or go back to the taxpayers who provided it in the first place.

I meant what I said. When the legislature didn't listen, I vetoed $213 million in spending. It sustained the vetoes of just $800,000 of it and spent the rest. In a Republican-controlled house and a Republican-controlled senate, no less! It just makes my point that we don't need Republican government, we need *conservative* government. My goal for the coming year is to get the legislature to understand how it is we got into this spending hole. Every dollar counts, and when we have extra ones, we should use them to pay down the debt or give them back to the taxpayers. If we don't, we risk becoming another Washington, D.C.—and in South Carolina, believe me, those are fighting words!

Another area where the establishment has struck back against my reform agenda has to do with something we in South Carolina call "restructuring." Restructuring is making government more efficient and more accountable—something we need to do in South Carolina almost as much as we need to do it in Washington, D.C. Our antiquated government structure features massive redundancy and waste. Every agency has its own e-mail server and its own back-office accounting and human resources department, among other inefficiencies.

Restructuring would streamline all that and put it into a Department of Administration that would be accountable to the governor. So in April we got legislation to do just that on the senate calendar. The senate kept telling me it would get to it, it would get to it, it would get to it . . . and then it didn't, and the session was scheduled to end on June 2. Publicly senators claimed to support the bill—who could be against less costly, more efficient government? But they had run out of time, darn the luck. The same thing had happened earlier with a similar restructuring bill supported by Governor Sanford. They wanted to pass it, they really did. They just ran out of time.

So I said, "You need more time? No problem." I issued an executive order to call the legislature back into session so it could finish its business. They didn't need to go home until they finished the work of the people of the state. For that I got sued by the Republican leader of the senate (if you haven't been able to keep track of the people who have sued me so far, here's the list: the unions, the ACLU, and an antireform Republican state senator. Not a bad record for my first year in office!). The lawsuit claimed that I could only call the legislature back into session in "extraordinary circumstances." The most amazing thing about it was that it admitted that the legislature not finishing its work wasn't extraordinary at all but, to quote the lawsuit, "the quintessential definition of an ordinary occurrence." In other words: Not getting their work done is business as usual. What would be "extraordinary" is if they did finish the job!

By just one vote, the South Carolina Supreme Court—the members of which, shockingly, are selected by the legislature—agreed with the antireform senator. The legislature did not come back into session. It did not finish its business. Life in Columbia proceeded as usual.

When I think about the restructuring fight, I think about the vision I had for South Carolina on my inauguration day: the vision of a government that works not for the best interests of itself but for the best interests of the people.

I still believe in that vision. I know the people of South Carolina do too. It's just going to take a little more work for me to persuade some of their elected officials to believe in it too.

Chapter Fourteen
Going Through the Burn

One of my favorite stories from being governor involves, of all things, a golf tournament.

For over forty years, Hilton Head has hosted the Heritage Golf Tournament. Over the years, golf legends like Arnold Palmer, Jack Nicklaus, and Greg Norman have played and won the Heritage. Each year some 135,000 fans pour into South Carolina, bringing in over eighty million dollars for our state. It's one of South Carolina's biggest sporting events and a stop on the PGA Tour. The Heritage is a big deal for us.

For years Verizon had been the Heritage's main corporate sponsor. But in 2009 the company announced that 2010 would be its last year sponsoring the tournament. The announcement set off a certain amount of Chicken Little behavior in South Carolina. As the months went by without finding a new sponsor, people who should have known better started acting like the sky was falling. Unless the taxpayers step in and pay for the tournament, they said, South Carolina will lose it.

That year a state house member from Beaufort County—the home county of the Heritage—sponsored a bill that would give ten million dollars in state funding to the tournament if it couldn't find a sponsor. The money would come from an insurance reserve fund set aside for hurricanes and other natural disasters.

Now, I love the Heritage. I love Hilton Head. My in-laws live there, and we spend every Thanksgiving, every Easter—and every Heritage golf tournament—on this island. And I love South Carolina's tourism industry. But we were in the middle of a budget crisis in 2010. We were laying off teachers, policemen, and social workers. Besides, even in prosperous times government has no business asking the taxpayers to pay for golf tournaments. And to raid an insurance trust fund to do it? So I fought the bill, against both Democrats and Republicans in the house.

The supporters of the bill said the money would only be spent if the Heritage couldn't find a sponsor. But that was precisely my point. We were giving the organizers of the tournament all the wrong incentives. We were encouraging them to look to government first when they should be scouring the private sector.

We successfully fought the bill in 2009, but the issue stayed with me as I campaigned for governor and the tournament failed to find a new sponsor. A government fix was a bad precedent for South Carolina. If we bailed out the golf tournament, there would be no end to the sporting events and festivals that would show up with their hands out. So when I took office, I announced that my number one priority in tourism was to find a private-sector sponsor for the Heritage. I didn't have one yet, but that year I went to the Heritage for the first time as governor and confidently told everyone that the tournament would have a private sponsor the following year. Just you wait and see! Again and again I told the media that allowing the Heritage to be sponsored by the taxpayers of South Carolina would kill it. The organizers would lose their ability to spend the way they wanted to. And what golf pro wants to play for a government golf tournament?

I was sticking my neck out, and I knew it. The Heritage was tapping its reserve fund to finance itself. If I didn't find a sponsor, in 2012 the only options would be to stick the taxpayers with the tab or turn the lights out on the tournament. Not to mention the fact that, if I lost the Heritage, I didn't know how Michael and I would be able to show our faces in Hilton Head that Thanksgiving. It was another one of those times where "can't" was just not an option.

I told my new director of tourism that his number one priority was to find a sponsor. I endlessly harangued my staff. I personally called company executives. We had dinners at the mansion to woo CEOs. A couple times we came close—once very close—only to have the deals fall apart at the last minute. But I never gave up.

Then, in June 2011, two months after the tournament had drained its reserves and when it looked like state funding was the only thing that could save it, we announced a sponsor. The Royal Bank of Canada (RBC) had agreed to sponsor the tournament for five years. Boeing had agreed to be the local sponsor. We had courted RBC hard, taking its executives to the tournament to see the players and meet the fans. It was on the second visit that they finally agreed. RBC's chief brand and communications officer told the newspapers the company had still been on the fence during one of my sales pitches when "she [Haley] looked at us, and I knew with that look there was no way we were getting off the bus."

I have to admit, it felt good. Not just to make good on my commitment but to see government work the way I believed it should work—the way I knew it could work in South Carolina. Too often government is lazy—and arrogant. It confronts a problem and takes the easy way out by throwing it back on the taxpayers. It's too hard or it takes too much time or it offends some special interest to find a real solution, so politicians go with a government solution, and the taxpayers end up paying for it. And if government isn't accountable to the people, it just keeps doing the lazy and arrogant thing and passing the buck to the taxpayers. That's what we had been about to do with the Heritage, and our state government's lack of initiative would have ruined a great South Carolina institution.

It's this same tendency that has gotten us into such a spending and debt hole in Washington. Whether it's a bank bailout, an auto bailout, a health-care bailout, or a golf bailout—it's all government being careless and unaccountable with the taxpayers' money. Take Obamacare. This was another case where government encountered a difficult problem and made it the taxpayers' problem. Yes, the plan speaks to its supporters' desire to grow government and exercise more control over our lives, but it's also just plain arrogant and lazy. Think about it this way: Every state in the country has serious issues with its Medicaid program, yet what's the biggest component of Obamacare? Forcing more Americans into Medicaid. How is our health-care problem solved by pushing more people into a government program that already doesn't work very well?

The truth is, nobody in the Obama administration knew how to fix things—at least, not how to fix them without alienating a bunch of special interests—so they took the easy way out and created more government and more government mandates. The same thing was true with the Obama stimulus bill. It's hard to cut spending—to live within your means when times are tough. So government tends to avoid making the tough calls. It all goes back to the Margaret Thatcher quote I used in my inaugural speech. Washington hasn't just accepted spending and taxes as a necessary evil; it has embraced them as a first resort. And our freedom has been damaged in the process.

Doing the hard thing—making the tough choices that are best for the taxpayers—is what I call "going through the burn." It's a term I learned from working in my mother's business. That's what Mom called it when the business suffered a downturn and we had to hunker down, cut back, and figure out what we needed to have to survive. When a business goes through the burn, the arrogance of profits goes away and certainty no longer exists. When a business goes through the burn, it gets smart and lean. It's forced to think about the long term. It's forced to prioritize if it wants to survive. I learned at an early age that the best decisions are made going through the burn. It focuses you on what's really important. You stop wasting time doing unproductive or unprofitable things. And when business picks up and money starts coming in again, you're more efficient and streamlined. You save and take precautions. You become a better businessperson.

Millions of American entrepreneurs do this every day—especially these days. A major source of the frustration Americans are feeling with Washington is that we don't understand why government can't—or won't—do the same thing. Every small businessman and businesswoman in America understands that the bottom line is the bottom line—you can't spend what you don't have, and you can only borrow so much. We understand that there are no magical rules that Washington lives by that make it immune to the same forces. Some people like to say that government has no bottom line, and that's why it borrows and spends the way it does. But that's not true. Government has limited resources just like the rest of us. It's just that when Washington exceeds those limits, it's us, the taxpayers, who pay.

Some think it's political suicide to talk too much about cutting back or going through the burn. But the American people are smarter than that, especially now. The fact is, government going through the burn is a lot like a business going through the burn: The result is a stronger, smarter, smaller, and more focused government. The difference is that the private sector is limited only by the creativity and hard work of entrepreneurs. The exact opposite is true in government. It was created to do the basics: secure the rights of the people, protect private property, provide for the common defense. In government, smaller is better.

I'm an accountant, so let's lay out the numbers. As of last fall, the national debt was $14.639 trillion. That's up $4 trillion from the $10.626 trillion in debt we had the day President Obama took office. That's the fastest increase in debt under any U.S. president. But President Obama just accelerated a dangerous trend. Our debt grew by $4.9 trillion under President George W. Bush. Thanks to the arrogance of both parties—thanks to politicians who lived for today and didn't think about the future for our children and grandchildren—our debt is now 97.6 percent of our gross domestic product, the total value of all the goods and services produced in the United States.

These numbers are scary, but I look at them and I see opportunity. There's no question that we can't go on spending like this. Something's got to give—either the government or the taxpayers. My feeling is, the government is the one that needs to change. It works for us after all. It's time for government to go through the burn.

We need a business plan for government, and a business plan begins with the basics: looking at every potential spending item and asking, "What's its function?" I fundamentally believe the role of government is to secure the rights and freedoms of the people. Government was never intended to be all things to all people. Redefining government will be hard, and it will involve difficult choices. But in the end we will have a government more like our founders intended it to be, more like the one we had when my parents gave up lives of wealth and privilege in India for a life of opportunity in America.

A business plan also has to consider the wants and needs of its customers, and our business plan for government won't succeed unless it does the same. Nothing will change until government is accountable to the people. That's what I love most about the Tea Party. It's drawing the line on government arrogance and overspending with the taxpayers' money. Whether it's in Columbia or in Washington, D.C., the Tea Party is saying to government: "We put you in office. We pay your salary. Figure it out. And the answer is not to turn around and ask us to pay for it. If you can't do it, we'll find someone who will."

Finally holding government accountable and breaking the spend-and-borrow cycle is why I worked with Texas governor Rick Perry to recruit other governors to support the "cut, cap and balance" plan in the debt-ceiling negotiations last summer. Governor Perry and I wrote an op-ed for the *Washington Post* in which we opposed an increase in the debt ceiling unless three commonsense things happened: First, we needed to have substantial cuts in spending. Otherwise, what was the point? Second, we needed to have enforceable spending caps to prevent Congress from spending extra revenues instead of using them to pay down the debt or returning them to the taxpayers. And third, we wanted to see congressional passage of a balanced-budget amendment to the U.S Constitution. The federal government should be forced to do what most of the fifty states already have to do.

We didn't get "cut, cap and balance." So what *did* we get? A whole lot of talk, some good intentions, but no resolution to our debt crisis. The debt-ceiling agreement negotiated between President Obama and the Congress was hailed as a great breakthrough. But let's be clear: It didn't fundamentally change anything. We increased the debt. We didn't freeze spending. We didn't balance the budget. And as an added bonus, we lost our AAA credit rating. How exactly is that a breakthrough?

A temporary budget fix is no fix at all. Government in its natural state is arrogant and lazy unless the people, to paraphrase Abraham Lincoln, save the government. In South Carolina we've won votes on the record and we're demanding new responsibility on the part of government with the taxpayers' money. We have to hold Washington similarly accountable. That means budget cuts now. A cap on all future spending. And a constitutionally mandated balanced budget from here on out.

My mother used to say that the best thing that can happen to a business is for the competition to open up across the street. When that happens, you come into work every day remembering who you're trying to serve, and you compete harder for their business. Government has no competition, of course. It is, as Mrs. Thatcher reminded us, a necessary evil. But we need to remember that we're its customers—and we need to make sure our elected officials remember that as well. It's our money. They work for us. When both sides are clear on that, we will have taken the first step to being the free, strong, and striving nation we were always meant to be.

The columnist George F. Will recently wrote: "If the question is which state has changed most in the last half-century, the answer might be California. But if the question is which state has changed most for the better, the answer might be South Carolina."

Will and other commentators have pointed to my and Tim Scott's elections as proof of how much has changed in South Carolina. As I've always said, there may be some truth to that. My election was important to discrediting one kind of racial politics. But it was also key in discrediting another kind of racial politics—one that I would argue is more prevalent today: the idea that for government to be legitimate, it has to "look like" the people it governs.

I don't look like many people in South Carolina. I won not on the color of my skin or the background of my parents but on the strength of my ideas. The dangerous idea that too often hides under the label of "diversity"—the notion that our leaders have to look like us in order for our voices to be heard—suffered a setback this past election. South Carolinians, it turns out, care more about accountability in government, creating jobs, and fighting bailouts than about racial politics.

I will be the first to say that we're not perfect. We haven't put bigotry and racism behind us completely. But we have avoided, for now at least, falling into the trap of trading one form of interest-group politics for another. Racial-identity politics may have had better intentions behind it than the good-old-boy system, but at root they both take power from the people and give it to the government. I've spent my life fighting against precisely that kind of politics. My parents came here to leave behind a culture and a political system that judges people by the family or the caste or the religion they come from. They came here because in America they would stand before the law and before government as individuals, not as members of a group. There were no guarantees. They might succeed and they might fail. But they wouldn't have the game rigged against them because of who they were. I owe them, and I owe my fellow South Carolinians, everything I have to continue to make good on that promise.

In a larger sense, this is what the Movement has always been about. It's about putting power back in the hands of the people. Not because we're saints but because we have a God-given right to our freedom, and freedom means the right to govern ourselves. It's when we have fallen short of this—when we've excluded certain groups from the full exercise of their freedom—that have been the times of our national shame.

There's not much doubt that the South Carolina of fifty years ago would not have elected me governor. Our little corner of America is truly an amazing place. We still have lots of serious problems, and I work on them every day. But we have made enormous progress. I see it with my own eyes all the time. You should come visit us and see for yourself. Better yet, you should move your family or your business here. As long as I'm governor, you'll be happy you did.

But I worry about our country. South Carolina, like every state, is not immune from the larger economic and political winds beyond our borders. What we're seeing today from Washington, D.C., is truly shocking and disturbing. Debt levels and deficits the size of which we've never seen before. Government-mandated health care that gets approved by Congress with one back-scratching deal after another. Enormous stimulus spending bills that reward political cronies instead of boosting our economy, while government bureaucrats tell companies they can't choose where to locate. It's the exact opposite of the movement for limited, responsible, and transparent government that I fight for in South Carolina.

I believe Americans fundamentally want to see people succeed. We want to succeed for ourselves and our families, but one of the great things about this country is that we understand that our neighbor's ability to get ahead is tied up with our own. We don't play class warfare politics very well here, and I love that. We don't want to see government take more from "the rich," because we all think we or our children can be rich someday, and in America we can.

Americans are increasingly demanding that their government do something different, rather than just avoiding the problem by throwing it back on the taxpayers. We've been down this road before. We know where it ends.

In the 1930s Americans suffered a Great Depression like none ever seen before or since. The national unemployment rate was 25 percent—25 percent!—and things weren't just bad here. Economic disaster of this type contributed to the rise of fascism in Europe. Terrible economic conditions helped bring communists to power in Russia a bit sooner and in China a bit later. For reasons that go deep into our national character and the brilliance of our founding system of government, Americans did not choose the totalitarian path. We chose to preserve our basic freedoms. But we did choose to change directions.

President Franklin Roosevelt's New Deal changed how Americans thought about the federal government. People were suffering, and the private sector was viewed as having failed. So the American people, under Roosevelt's direction, turned to government. It was a government that appeared more compassionate and caring but was at the same time more aggressive and intrusive.

Some of the government interventions of that time and of the previous progressive era are things we now take for granted. Social Security as a way to reduce rampant poverty among the elderly. Child labor laws and minimum-wage and maximum-work-hour laws to curb some of the roughest edges of the capitalist system. The ability to *voluntarily* join an industrial labor union. We would no more look to undo these innovations than we would seek to return to the pre–civil rights era laws on race discrimination. They have become a part of the American fabric, and it's a good thing they have.

But the New Deal and the array of big government programs centralized in Washington that sprang up in the decades that followed have brought our country to a different place. The modern welfare state has bred dependency, debt, and economic stagnation. We've lost a lot of that "don't complain, do something about it" spirit that my parents worked so hard to teach us as kids. In exchange for dubious promises of comfort and security, we've surrendered too much of our freedom to government.

Now we are faced with another major economic crisis. To be sure, it hasn't reached the level of the Great Depression; but it is nonetheless large enough in its scope, reach, and despair to get Americans to once again examine our fundamental assumptions about what the federal government ought to do. It's got us thinking about what our government could be if we just went through the burn.

President Obama's approach is to avoid the burn, to mimic the New Deal by spending more, going further into debt, and creating more centralized government command and control. Instead of rallying us all to succeed and offering the "hope" he proclaimed as a candidate, he's dialed up the class warfare rhetoric in an attempt to divide us.

The problem for Obama, however, is that he is using the New Deal playbook absent the conditions that made the New Deal possible. We have now had some seventy-five years of federal-government growth, and we can see where it's brought us. We see the federal government bailing out Wall Street banks and auto companies at taxpayers' expense and picking winners and losers in the marketplace. We see federal dominance of the mortgage-lending business and an ensuing housing catastrophe. We see a federal takeover of health care and know the disaster that awaits.

It is quite simply no longer credible for Washington politicians to claim, as they credibly did in the 1930s, that more intervention from Washington is the solution to our problems. If Washington does such an abysmal job of managing its own finances, then why would anyone trust it to manage their health care? What's more, if a bigger, more bureaucratic, more intrusive federal government were the way to fix the economy, we would never have a recession to begin with, because Lord knows we've had a lot of big, intrusive government. The American people grasp this at a very gut level because they have now witnessed it for most of their lives.

Washington today is trying to lead America in one direction, but there is a growing understanding that a change is needed, and it needs to go in the opposite direction. Just as the excesses that led to the Great Depression gave rise to public support for much broader government interventionism in the 1930s, the excesses of today's uncontrolled, inefficient, and corrupt federal government are giving rise to support for a new direction that is marked by a more limited government with more transparency and accountability. There is a wave building in places like Madison and Trenton. In Columbia we call it the Movement. But whatever name it travels under, I pity the politicians who are on the wrong side of it.

In my lifetime I have seen the wondrous changes that the human condition can inspire when it is allowed to be free. When the daughter of Indian immigrants, who grew up in a small rural town in the segregated South, can become the first female and minority governor of her state and the youngest governor in the nation, then it's clear that the American Dream still exists. When the people start demanding that their governments rein in debt and regulations and operate honestly and transparently, as they have done in South Carolina and in much of the country, then you know our future will be great. It's a beautiful thing.

Yes, we have challenges. But I have great faith that this will all sort itself out for the better. Ask me about my faith in a rising, shining America, and the answer is never in doubt. For my country—just as for me—"can't" is not an option.

ACKNOWLEDGMENTS

In writing this book, just as in meeting all the challenges and having all the adventures it describes, I am thankful, first and foremost, to my family. My parents and brothers and sister were irreplaceably helpful in going back in time with me to tell the story of the Original Six. My husband, Michael, who has been my best friend and partner in these adventures, was also an indispensable writing partner. Thank you to Michael and to all my family for reliving our story together. We have been through a lot and it was fun going back and bringing it all back to life. Our children, Rena and Nalin, did their part by making us smile every day.

I want to thank Tim Pearson and Jon Lerner for the time and effort they gave in helping me with this project. Your friendship and guidance, personally and professionally, is invaluable and I will forever be grateful to both of you.

Thank you to Team Haley for the stories, the laughs, and the support throughout this journey. Taylor Hall, Rebecca Schimsa, Jeff Taillon, Madison Walker, Josh Baker, Rob Godfrey, Zach Pippin, Trey Walker, and Marisa Crawford . . . we did this. This is our story. I hope you will always be as proud of what we accomplished as I am.

Acknowledgments

My sincere thanks to Nick Ayers for caring enough to support someone that "should win," not just someone who "could win." Your friendship and professional support throughout this process will never be forgotten.

Bob Barnett, you're one of the coolest guys I have ever met. Thank you for your support of this project.

Words cannot describe what a pleasure it was to work with Jessica Gavora on this book. Jessica, you helped me stay true to who I am in writing this book. It was, at times, a painful process but in the end, it was a lot of fun. I can't imagine having worked with anyone else on this very personal book.

Thank you to Adrian Zackheim and the amazing people at Penguin who gracefully made sure all our t's were crossed and i's were dotted and still helped get this project done on time. It has been a real pleasure working with all of you.

Last, thank you to the wonderful people in the small town of Bamberg and across the state of South Carolina. You continue to give me faith in the goodness of the American people. I am thankful for the lessons, the support, and the inspiration you have always provided. You are what inspires me to live a life in which can't is not an option.

Notes

Chapter One: Bamberg

16   *a reporter from the* New York Times: Shaila Dawan and Robbie Brown, "All Her Life, Nikki Haley Was the Different One," *New York Times*, June 13, 2010.

Chapter Three: Nikki Who?

44   *He came upon a book*: Ross Petras and Kathryn Petras, *The Stupidest Things Ever Said by Politicians* (New York: Pocket Books, 1999), p. 38.

56   *"I have very little reason"*: Tim Flach, "Haley Overcomes Koon in GOP Runoff," *State*, June 23, 2004.

57   *Under the headline*: Brad Warthen, "Voters Embraced American Dream in Choosing Nikki Haley," *State*, June 27, 2004.

Chapter Four: The Good Old Boys' Club

66   *I finally got the proof*: South Carolina Policy Council, "South Carolina General Assembly Should Call Roll," August 5, 2008, available at http://scpolicycouncil.com/images/pdf/109.pdf.

70   *"I went against the Speaker"*: Jim Davenport, "SC House Speaker: It's Nothing Personal," Associated Press, December 4, 2008.

71 *At the* State, *Brad Warthen*: Brad Warthen, "Well I Guess He Showed Them Who the Big Ol' Hairy Speaker Is," TheState.com, December 5, 2008.

Chapter Five: Are They Ready?

86 *I was "a relative unknown"*: John O'Connor, "Haley Tries to Be 1st Woman to Lead S.C.," *State*, May 15, 2009.

86 *CNN reported that I would*: Peter Hamby, "Top Sanford Ally Enters Race for South Carolina Governor," CNNPolitics.com, May 14, 2009, http://politicalticker.blogs.cnn.com/2009/05/14/top-sanford-ally-enters-race-for-south-carolina-governor/.

86 Roll Call, *the Capitol Hill newspaper, got right to the point*: "Haley Officially in S.C. Governor's Race," *Roll Call*, May 14, 2009.

86 *While stopping short of endorsing*: CNNPolitics.com.

Chapter Six: The Sanford Implosion

89 *Jenny Sanford changed her tone*: Ali Velshi, Mike Brooks, Candy Crowley, Brooke Anderson, Larry King, CNN Newsroom, June 23, 2009.

91 *series of ill-advised interviews*: Tamara Lush and Evan Berland, "SC Gov Says Mistress is Soul Mate," Associated Press, June 30, 2009.

91 *The* State *gleefully published*: "Exclusive: Read E-mails Between Sanford, Woman," *State*, June 25, 2009.

96 *the impeachment bandwagon really gained*: Jim Rutenberg and Robbie Brown, "Governor Used State's Money to Visit Lover," *New York Times*, June 25, 2009.

Chapter Seven: Underdog

107 *In typical Sanford fashion*: Peter Hamby, "Sanford Blasts Investigator for 'Selective Outrage,' " CNNPolitics.com, August 27, 2009, http://politicalticker.blogs.cnn.com/2009/08/27/sanford-blasts-investigator-for-selective-outrage/.

108   *"I need this guy [Sanford] out"*: Shaila Dewan and Jim Rutenberg, "South Carolina Politics Looks Past Affair to Its Effects on Governor Race," *New York Times*, June 28, 2009.

108   *Back in 2003 a police*: Jack Kuenzie, "Lt. Gov. Bauer Caught Twice for Speeding Recently, Got No Tickets," Associated Press, WISTV.com, March 28, 2006.

117   *On November 11 she issued*: http://multimedia.augusta.com/video/news/2009/11/111009JennySanfordLetter.pdf.

Chapter Eight: Turning Points

120   *He once compared the government*: Nathaniel Cary, "Bauer: Needy 'Owe Something Back' for Aid," *State*, January 23, 2010.

120   *In another debate he famously*: Jim Davenport, Associated Press, April 24, 2010.

121   *As of March, the Rasmussen*: "McMaster Leads GOP Candidates," *State*, March 10, 2010.

125   *The next day the local paper*: "Best & Worst," *State*, January 29, 2010.

Chapter Nine: The Palin Effect

143   *The Rasmussen Poll showed*: "Poll: Haley Leads GOP Rivals," *Herald-Journal*, May 20, 2010.

Chapter Ten: Blood Sport

155   *She titled it*: Sarah Palin's Facebook page, May 24, 2010. http://www.facebook.com/note.php?note_id=392492378434.

161   *That Friday, June 4*: Seanna Adcox, Associated Press, June 4, 2010.

Chapter Eleven: Mandate

174   *The chamber's CEO*: Jim Davenport, Associated Press, July 8, 2010.

178   *In mid-October, three weeks*: Robert Behre, "New Polling Gives Haley 9-Point Lead," *Post and Courier*, October 13, 2010.

Chapter Twelve: Transition

187 *When the* Spartanburg Herald-Journal: Robert Ariail, "Hitt Man," *Spartanburg Herald–Journal*, December 10, 2010.

188 *Lillian Koller had led*: Yvonne Wenger, "Haley Appoints Social Service Head," *Post and Courier*, January 13, 2011.

189 *One black caucus member scolded*: Kris Hummer and Robert Kittle, WSAV.com, January 28, 2011, http://www2.wsav.com/news/2011/jan/28/gov-haleys-cabinet-diversity-controversy-ar-1397778/.

189 *After our closed-door meeting*: Gina Smith, "Haley Completes Cabinet; Diversity Questioned," *State*, January 29, 2011.

191 *In an article in the* Atlantic: Hanna Rosen, "Good Ol' Girl," *Atlantic*, January/February 2010.

Chapter Thirteen: The First 250 Days

208 *Judge Vinson's ruling should be*: Kevin Sack, "Federal Judge Rules That Health Law Violates Constitution," *New York Times*, January 31, 2011.

211 *Out of the more than*: Yvonne Wenger, "Illegal Immigration Law Impeded, Governor Says," *Post and Courier*, May 28, 2011.

212 *South Carolina experienced*: "Illegal Immigrants Expanding Footprint," Associated Press, *USA Today*, March 29, 2006.

212 *The Mexican drug cartels*: U.S. Department of Justice National Drug Intelligence Center, "Situation Report: Cities in Which Mexican DTOs Operate Within the United States," April 11, 2008, available at http://www.justice.gov/ndic/pubs27/27986/27986p.pdf.

214 *The machinists had struck*: Eric Pryne, "Boeing to Fight NLRB Complaint on 787 South Carolina Plant," *Seattle Times*, April 20, 2011.

214 *The lawsuit cited comments*: Letter from Boeing Executive Vice President and General Counsel J. Michael Luttig to Lafe E. Solomon, Acting General Counsel, National Labor Relations Board, May 3, 2011, available at http://seattletimes.nwsource.com/ABPub/2011/05/04/2014962951.pdf.

214 *The complaint also referred*: Joshua Freed, Associated Press, April 20, 2011.

215 *The company had predicted*: Jonathan Serrie, "BMW Gives Big Boost to South Carolina in Expansion of Assembly Plant," FoxNews.com, October 13, 2010, available at http://www.foxnews.com/us/2010/10/13/bmw-gives-big-boost-south-carolina-workforce-expansion-assembly-plant/.

216 *At the same time that*: Seattle Times.

217 *Their spokesman told the press*: "Haley Prompts Lawsuit: Union Goes to Court over Boeing Plant Comments," *Post and Courier*, January 21, 2011.

219 *The Small Business Administration estimates*: Nicole V. Crain and W. Mark Crain, "The Impact of Regulatory Costs on Small Firms," Small Business Administration Office of Advocacy, September 2010, available at http://archive.sba.gov/advo/research/rs371tot.pdf.

Chapter Fourteen: Going Through the Burn

225 *Each year some 135,000 fans*: The Heritage, "The Tradition Continues," http://www.theheritagegolfsc.com/8_history.php.

227 *RBC's chief brand and communications officer*: Robert Behre, "Saving the Heritage: Haley's Involvement Kept Tournament Alive in S.C.," *Post and Courier*, July 4, 2011.

230 *As of last fall*: Mark Knoller, "National Debt Has Increased $4 Trillion Under Obama," CBSNews.com, August 22, 2011, http://www.cbsnews.com/8301-503544_162-20095704-503544.html?tag=cbsnewsMainColumnArea.

232 *The columnist George F. Will*: George F. Will, "As GOP Diversifies, South Carolina Is Rising," *Washington Post*, September 9, 2010.